| LEARNING |
| TO SAY NO |

Establishing Healthy Boundaries

Carla Wills-Brandon

AN AUTHORS GUILD BACKINPRINT.COM EDITION

Learning To Say No:
Establishing Healthy Boundaries
All Rights Reserved © 1990, 2000 by Carla Wills-Brandon

AN AUTHORS GUILD BACKINPRINT.COM EDITION

Published by iUniverse.com, Inc.

For information address:
iUniverse.com, Inc.
620 North 48th Street, Suite 201
Lincoln, NE 68504-3467
www.iuniverse.com

Originally published by Health Communications, Inc Deerfield Beach, Florida

ISBN: 0-595-09351-5

Printed in the United States of America

I DEDICATION I

This book is dedicated to all of the Carlas who live within me.

I ACKNOWLEDGMENTS I

Another book is born and its completion has been made possible by many more than meet the eye.

Michael, my mate in recovery, was the unfortunate guinea pig who first experienced many of the boundary exercises presented in this book. I love and appreciate his willingness to explore one more area of growth with me.

My son Aaron also contributed greatly to this book, even though he was only three years of age at the time it was evolving. He taught me about the word *no* and demonstrated how it could be used in a variety of situations. His ability to say *no* taught me that to set boundaries is a basic human right that most of us were not allowed.

Rita Baker once again did a bang-up job typing the overwhelming number of hand-written pages which have evolved into the text of this book. I know reading through my scrawling isn't easy and her talents are greatly appreciated.

Marie Stilkind, my editor, is a dear friend who gave this work the polish that it needed for success. I will always value her creativity and her friendship.

I would also like to thank the entire Health Communications and U.S. Journal family, along with the crowd at the Diane Glynn agency for the work they have done in promoting me as an author. I appreciate the risks that have been taken on my behalf.

Finally, I need to express my appreciation to all of the family, friends, clients and peers who have not only provided me with many situations for setting boundaries but who have also been willing to risk and set boundaries with me. Thanks to all who have given me an opportunity to learn how to take care of myself in healthy ways, as opposed to depending on those dysfunctional survival skills I learned during childhood.

I CONTENTS I

I INTRODUCTION I

Hello, my name is Carla, and I am recovering from the first half of my life. The recovery process has been a rewarding, and yet at the same time, curious experience. Before entering my recovery I had spent thousands of dollars and many hours in traditional psychotherapy trying to figure out what was wrong with me. I had always felt as if I had a screw loose somewhere in my being and was constantly looking for that one drug, therapist, classroom experience, workshop, encounter group or guru that could repair me. I felt so damaged and hopeless, wishing only to feel a part of the human race.

I wanted specific answers to my problem or, better yet, a "Big Fix" that would make me feel complete. Grasping after anything, I was looking for some hint to my dilemma such as, "If you do this the result will be . . . *and poof* . . . you will find your true self and live happily ever after." It sounded easy enough, but it sure felt beyond my reach. I felt as if I had been set aside from the rest of humankind to be miserable for life.

Therapy started at age 19 with traditional psychotherapy. I was concerned about my drinking because it reminded me of my mother's. I was assured my drinking wasn't a problem and was promptly subjected to hypnosis.

Thinking maybe my subconscious mind would give me some answers, I was a very willing subject. But my cure wasn't there, most likely because I was a full-blown alcoholic and under the influence at times during therapy sessions. This probably attributed to the ease to which I was hypnotized.

When traditional psychotherapy didn't appear to work, it was suggested I try Valium. I said no thank you because a number of women in my family of origin had been addicted to the drug. It was then suggested I try Ativan. I had never heard of Ativan and thought, why not? Maybe this was the magic potion I needed. The tranquilizer Ativan proved to be Valium's sister and very addictive. Ativan mixed with booze depressed me even more, and I was disappointed that my fantasy about this little pill was truly a myth.

Eventually, another helping professional suggested I try the latest thing on the market for my "blues." This little bit of magic, he stated, was called an antidepressant. He also assured me that these pretty blue pills were not addictive. My blue pills made me feel "null and void," and I never felt like I was really in my body. I was positive that antidepressants were not my cure but decided to mix them with the Ativan and alcohol anyway. By the way, my body had the most difficult time detoxing off the antidepressants while in treatment for chemical dependency.

One day, in a fit of rage, I cried out, "Why am I so screwed up?", hoping God or somebody would answer me with a burning bush, lightning bolt, postcard or some type of sign which would place me squarely on the golden road toward inner peace. Well, I never did see a burning bush or get a postcard from God, but I did eventually discover I was an alcoholic, drug addict, food addict, codependent, love addict with a set of lifeskills that were useless. I also discovered that, along with all of my active addictions, my concepts and fantasies about life all came from my family of origin and the television set, neither of which was very healthy.

Slowly, one by one, I began letting go of the chemical addictions. After I achieved sobriety from pills and booze, my brain started to defrost. I noticed the sky was blue, my eyes were green and that I had a strong desire to learn about life. Next I found recovery for my eating disorder. After being out of touch with my body for so many years, I began to really feel in my body and discovered my physical appearance was not so bad after all. As time went on, I learned how to love my height of six feet and my size 11 shoe size.

Eventually, I said good-bye to cigarettes. I had a funeral for my last pack of cigarettes and also for my ashtrays, lighters and matches. Though I knew it was time to let go of this addiction, I felt some sadness as I flushed the last five cigarettes down the toilet. Nicotine had enabled me to suppress my feelings of anger and fear during a time when I was not capable of learning from them. As I progressed in my own process of self-discovery, I learned I needed to experience anger and fear for my own growth.

Two years into my own recovery I felt overwhelmed. I didn't have any more chemicals to hide behind. I felt alone and vulnerable without protection. Memories from childhood began to make their presence known in my dreams, reactions to others, behavior at work and with family. Vivid memories of emotional, physical and sexual abuse began to surface and haunt me like clips from an old horror movie. At times I really thought I was going crazy and questioned why I had given up all of those mood-altering chemicals.

I began to respond to scenes on television. My body would freeze up if a sexually abusive scene was displayed on television, or I would burst out crying if the scene involved loud fighting. At the time, I had no idea that what I was seeing and hearing on television had happened to me and that my body was remembering, even though my mind had forgotten.

With these overwhelming feelings, the next phase of my recovery from the first half of my life began. I started exploring how I had grown up, what my family of origin was like and how I had been abused.

I discovered, with a great deal of patient help, that I had been very abused in a number of ways. So I beat on pillows, threw old mayonnaise jars and raged at those who abused me. I even yelled at God and the universe for the pain I had experienced as a child. I wrote letters to those who had abandoned me and confronted others who had hurt my body, heart and soul. I grieved with several of the inner children who were hiding within me, and I learned how to nurture myself and them. I grieved deeply for the myths I had about my childhood as I let go of them one by one.

I also went searching for God. I had been raised with a very scary concept of an abusive punishing God. The God I was raised with kept score and didn't protect me. This God had the characteristics of those who had abused me and was not a safe concept of a Higher Power for me to hold on to. So — I fired this concept and began my quest for a healthy concept of God.

I wanted a Higher Power that would protect me but at the same time not keep me isolated from life. I wanted a God that would not expect me to view myself as above or better than others, but at the same time did not require that I live my life as a doormat. I wanted a Higher Power that would teach me how to be of service to others but not to the extent of co-dependent behavior. I wanted a God that would allow me to set limits with others in a healthy tactful manner as opposed to being abusive or hurtful to others. I wanted a Higher Power to teach me how to grow up and take care of myself responsibly.

What I discovered was that what I was really looking for was not God so much as it was boundaries or healthy living skills for self-protection. I wanted to know how to take care of myself with healthy responsible adult behavior. I wanted to know how to feel safe and at the same time not isolated in all situations. I went to a lecture on boundaries, hoping I would finally find the answer to my quest. I even asked the lecturer if it was possible to buy boundaries somewhere from a workshop or class. What I discovered was that acquiring boundaries came from trial and error and a lot of hard work. What that meant was more self-exploration and growing.

This book is about healthy personal power and healthy boundaries. Many of us come from families where we were not taught about our own personal power. Healthy personal power gives us permission to take care of ourselves, allows us to set up healthy boundaries to protect us in all situations. Healthy personal power gives us the ability to be responsible for ourselves and our well-being.

As a consequence of growing up with addiction in our family of origin, we were disempowered by certain types of abuse. As disempowered individuals we do not know how to take care of ourselves, believing our needs are not important, that our opinions should not be expressed. We rarely say no and fear the word selfish. We seldom feel safe and constantly feel victimized.

What we do know how to do with expert skill is take care of others. We put the needs of others before our own in hopes of being accepted and loved. Much of the time we end up feeling abused, used and unappreciated. Many helping professionals call this co-dependent behavior.

Others of us have an overwhelming unhealthy sense of power. There is a feeling of invincibility, and the need for control is all-consuming. Individuals with an overdeveloped sense of power were given too much of it as children in their family of origin. There is a sense that the need for control borders on a need for survival and that to be out of control risks an inability to survive.

For those of us who have been overempowered, it is difficult, if not impossible, to share who we really are. Our boundaries are thick brick barriers that we hide behind. These barriers look perfect on the outside and give a false sense of our state of being to those around us, while on the inside, we are frightened, alone and in pain. Overempowered individuals, like disempowered individuals, have suffered emotional, physical and/or sexual abuse within their family of origin. Those of us who have been disempowered have difficulty feeling safe because we haven't the tools necessary to protect ourselves. While those of us who are overempowered only feel safe behind lonely isolating thick walls of addiction or distancing behaviors.

The majority of us swing from having no boundaries or sense of safety to the extreme of putting up barriers in order to attain a feeling of security. Living life from one extreme to another can be painful, frustrating and confusing.

An example of this would be of a young woman who has one dysfunctional relationship after another. Upon entering a new relationship, the excitement and intensity brings a false sense of hope that "this is the one." She hopes and prays for Mr. Right to come along and make her complete. She wants respect, intimacy and security but constantly finds herself in abusive relationships. She is aware that all of her relationship mates have the characteristics of her alcoholic father, but is frustrated with this repeated pattern. After each relationship, hurt and angry, she emotionally puts herself down for picking out the same abusive type to have a relationship with. She vows to avoid all men and live a life of celibacy.

One day, realizing she is very lonely, she decides to try dating again. Within six months to a year, she finds herself once again in an incredibly dysfunctional relationship. This woman moves from not having protective boundaries that provide awareness and safety, to building walls of isolation and hiding out after experiencing pain.

Many of us can only experience so much pain before we shut down emotionally, socially and at times even physically. This is how we survived in family systems which were dysfunctional. Small children who are emotionally, physically or sexually abused learn very early on how to detach from the pain of abuse. They learn how to unconsciously numb their bodies while being abused. This is why most abuse survivors have extensive memory loss. They move from being totally exposed and vulnerable to being isolated within walls of numbness.

Consequences to disempowerment or overempowerment during childhood disrupt adulthood, making it difficult to establish healthy responsible boundaries. Since most of us came from families where it was difficult to feel emotionally, physically or sexually safe, we have become involved in a number of addictions and dysfunctional behaviors which give us a false sense of security. I have always believed addiction was a type of surrogate parenting which initially provided a feeling of false security.

Eventually, though, these addictions and dysfunctional behaviors backfire and keep us from evolving into the healthy, spiritual beings we were meant to be. Our concepts about personal power become intermingled with our addictions and self-defeating behaviors. We live life to the extreme in relation to our boundaries and personal power. We may have a sense of being less than those around us: less attractive, less intelligent, less lovable. We may feel we need to be in control, on top of the heap and better than those around us at all costs.

Eventually, after much hard work, I did learn what healthy boundaries were. Today I don't have to be totally exposed and victimized. Nor do I need to isolate and avoid the life experience. I can take care of myself, fulfill my needs, state my opinions and stand by my values without being a wet doormat or rigid hardnose.

It is my hope that you, the reader, will take from this book that which applies to your life and feels right for your own personal journey. I believe the life experience is supposed to be about discovering who we really are. Unfortunately, most of us did not receive the tools necessary for a successful journey. Many of us have conquered addiction and worked diligently on our own unfinished business only to feel somehow incomplete. We have gone to recovery programs, participated in workshops, beaten on pillows and been in therapy for what seems like a lifetime, only to continue asking ourselves, "How come I still feel so insecure and unsafe? Why is trust in myself and others so hard?" or, as I asked over and over again, "Where is the big fix, the magical potion, the final cure that is going to pull it all together?"

My answers came to me with continual self-exploration. Our answers eventually must come from within if they are truly to be ours. This is how we discover who we really are, the purpose of existence, the meaning of life and our own spirituality. Since I so strongly believe it is important for you to discover your own answers, I have included a workbook section at the end of the book. This section provides suggestions and directions for discovery of healthy personal power and the establishment of healthy boundaries. We all have a right to feel we are grown up enough and confident enough to take care of ourselves in healthy ways. It is my hope that you will discover that you are not only your own best friend, but also your own best parent.

Good luck to you on your journey.

Carla Wills-Brandon

The Family Of Origin
And Boundary Development | 1

When my son Aaron was 18 months old, he added a new word to his vocabulary. That word was *no!* Every other sentence had the word *no* in it. As he grew older the word *no* became even more assertive.

"No! I don't want to eat that!"

"No, I don't want to take a bath!"

"No! I want to wear the green shirt, not the blue one!"

"No! I want to play with Daddy, not Mama!"

My child was learning how to set boundaries, and I was amazed how easy it was for him to do this. He was also making choices, and he even started expressing himself with comments like,"I'm mad at you, Mama . . . Grandma's sad today . . . Mama loves me." I found this rather amazing. The word *no* was unacceptable in my family of origin, and I learned it very early on. Words expressing anger and sadness were viewed as negative and inappropriate. As I watched my son grow, I realized we were supposed to begin learning about boundaries and personal power at a very early age.

9

When children reach approximately one year of age, they are usually mobile. They can crawl around and are learning how to walk. Before this, children are completely dependent on their parents for their very survival. During infancy, children cannot see themselves as separate entities. They view themselves as a part of their parents. As they move through the toddler years, they begin to see that they are separate from their parents and begin to explore themselves and the world around them. They explore what they hear, see and feel with a myriad of questions: "Daddy, is it raining outside? . . . Mama, is that color blue? . . . Daddy, is Mama sad? . . . Mama, is Daddy at the office? . . . Mama, is Grandma tired? . . . Daddy, did the man on TV die?" Children need to have their reality validated in order to grow into healthy adults who can trust their own perceptions.

Personal Power

Another popular word during the toddler years is *mine*. "This is *my* blanket, Mama . . . This is *my* gum, Daddy . . . This is *my* room, Grandpa . . . This is *my* bed, Grandma . . . These are *my* fingers and toes, Daddy." Toddlers begin to realize they are separate beings and that certain things belong to them. As separate entities they begin to demand their personal space and privacy.

At age two and a half Aaron wanted to bathe himself and began pushing me out of the bathroom when he needed to use the toilet. "I can do it, Mama! . . . Let me do it."

Children begin exploring their own personal power, which teaches them how to take care of themselves. Exploring personal power builds confidence and self-esteem, and teaches children about success and failure. Success feels good and teaches children how to feel good about their own accomplishments. Failure is a teacher which gives children permission to be childlike, imperfect and human. Success builds confidence in personal power while failure teaches it's all right to make a mistake and that mistakes do not decrease personal power.

When children are emotionally, physically or sexually abused by adults, they are disempowered and in many cases empowered. We will discuss this later but for the time being, let's continue looking at how children learn.

Parent Power

Children's first concept of God or a Higher Power doesn't come from their parents' religious preference, it comes more directly from the behavior of the parents. Children see their parents as all-knowing and godlike. Physically, parents are big, and children depend on their parents for their very survival. Parents are supposed to provide food, clothing, shelter, nurturing, healthy physical touch, medical attention, safety and a healthy set of tools and concepts for understanding the world. Parents naturally are in a very delicate position of power. When children are raised with healthy parents, their concept of God and their world around them is balanced and healthy. They grow into adults who have a healthy set of tools for living independently on their own upon reaching adulthood. A child experiments within his or her family of origin in order to prepare for the adult world. Children learn how to feel about themselves by watching how their parents treat them and each other.

Learning About Anger

In my family of origin the men were always in charge and won all of the disagreements in the household. The women in my family were passive and had difficulty being direct with their anger. It was acceptable for men to be angry but the women, when angered, would express it indirectly by overcharging on credit cards or cooking a lousy meal. I grew up believing it was not "ladylike" to be angry and that being angry was a "male thing." So when angry with my husband, Michael, instead of being direct, I would burn food or overcharge on credit cards. This made sense to me. To this day, there are times when I will be angry with someone and burn a meal before realizing I need to be direct with my anger.

Children model their behavior after their parents' behavior. Michael and I enjoy golf, and we take our son, Aaron, golfing with us. Michael periodically becomes angered with his golf swing and will mumble a few swear words upon missing a shot. He also rocks back and forth on his feet before he swings his club to hit the ball. One day I was watching Aaron, who was three years of age at the time, hit his ball. I began to notice he would rock back and forth on his feet before swinging his club and upon missing the swing, he would swear. Aaron was learning about being male by watching his father. Needless to say, Michael began watching his vocabulary on the golf course.

Children learn what it means to be male by watching male family members. Likewise they learn what it means to be female by watching the women in the family. Also children learn about relationships by watching their parents interact with one another. They learn about the world by living in the world of the family. They learn about traditions, values, prejudices, beliefs and more from their parents, believing these traditions and values are right, even if they are dysfunctional, simply because parents are in a position of authority. Children believe their parents must be right because they are parents. Children will also believe their parents are right even if their intuition says otherwise. Because children see their parents as godlike, children will trust their parents' perception before they will trust their own.

JOE'S STORY | Joe's father never appeared to become angry. Everybody in Joe's family would talk about how "in control" and "solid" Joe's father was. They would also tell Joe that his father was a wonderful man, that the family counted on him for stability. Joe's mother was very emotional and would cry a lot. When she did this, Joe's father seemed to take it in stride. Family members would say Joe's mother was very lucky to have Joe's father for a husband. While playing baseball one day, Joe fell down and hurt himself. His knee was bleeding, and he felt the pain of torn skin. He really wanted to cry, but didn't because in his family only women cried. Joe learned how to numb out physical pain over time.

During his teenage years, Joe enjoyed snow skiing with his friends. Every weekend he and his friends would pile into his old truck and head for the ski slopes in the high California mountains. One day while skiing, Joe caught his leg on a tree limb buried under the snow while he was going down a ski slope. His shin began to swell up, so he packed it in snow. One of his friends found him sitting in the snow and asked, "Are you all right? Would you like me to find the ski patrol to help you down the mountain?" But Joe replied, "Oh no! I'm fine. Let's go ski some more." By the end of the day, Joe's leg was very swollen and purple. On the way back home, Joe asked his friends to stop at a liquor store so he could get some beer to dull the pain in his leg. Several weeks later, Joe ended up in the emergency room and had to have surgery on his leg. Joe had grown up not trusting the feeling of emotional or physical pain.

Teacher

Our pain tells us when something is wrong so that we can take care of ourselves. Our pain is a signal to us that it is time to take action to protect ourselves. By taking action we are being responsible and setting boundaries for ourselves. If Joe had had healthy boundaries, he would have acknowledged the pain in his leg, asked for help down the mountain and gone to the hospital. Both emotional and physical pain are clues to us that something within us is in need of healing. If we shut that pain off by numbing it out, or with addiction, we can never heal.

Pain is a teacher which motivates us to become responsible for ourselves. It also provides us with a direct message that states, "There is need for resolution, for healing and growth." Most of us come from families where we have learned that if you tough it out and ignore it, it will go away.

When I was newly sober, my ability to set boundaries with others was extremely difficult. People would constantly borrow money from me and not pay it back. I would lend my emotional support, time and material possessions to people who did not give of themselves in return. I felt like I was the caretaker who was always victimized and wondered why I felt so used in my friendships.

My family believed in the phrase "Don't be selfish," and lived by this principle. My mother's mother was constantly doing for others. She took care of everyone in need, even when she herself was in poor health. Not only was she a professional nurse in a local hospital, but she also nursed friends, relatives and more on her time off. She believed a positive attitude was necessary at all costs, but her own physical illnesses were stress-related. Grandmother would never take time out for her own healing. In physical pain, she would put a smile on her face and take a pie or casserole to a sick neighbor. My grandmother could never say no to anybody.

Grandma's father was an alcoholic and gambler who had abandoned her and her sister for her mother's best friend. My grandmother always had a fear of being alone and abandoned. Her first born, my uncle, was killed during World War II in Germany. My grandmother never healed from her grief over this loss. Her second child, my mother, died at the age of 37 from cancer. I remember my grandmother at my mother's funeral saying, "Keep a positive attitude." My grandfather had been crippled throughout my lifetime, and my grandmother busied herself with his needs when not caretaking others. My grandmother never addressed any of her losses. She covered up her pain by doing, doing, doing for others.

Disempowerment

What I learned watching all of this as a small child was that *no* was a "sinful" word and not to do for others when asked was unacceptable. I remember at an early age believing it was selfish to think of myself before others. I truly believed God would not like me if I was selfish and had a fear I would be punished. I grew up with two younger sisters, and my grandmother would always say, "Carla,

always think about them before you think about yourself."
When my mother died, I didn't cry. I was told I needed to
be strong for my sisters because they were younger.

I was disempowered by being told I should not have my
feelings of pain, anger and grief. I was told it was selfish
for me to have my feelings and that I needed to be in
control. I remember feeling like I was really weak and
selfish because I wanted to just break down and cry in
somebody's arms with the pain I felt about the loss of my
mother. At the same time I was also being empowered
because it was expected of me to behave like an adult and
when I did so, I was praised. I was given the role of
surrogate mother over my sisters and this put me in a
position of authority and power. Now that my mother
was dead, I was told I was in charge. One can imagine the
feelings of grandiosity a 16-year-old would have being
given such a position.

Needing To Be Needed

In treatment in early sobriety I feared being known as
selfish by my peers. So like my grandmother I would do,
do, do for anyone who asked. I would bake cookies, drive
people wherever they wanted to go. (I once took a woman
to visit her daughter who lived out of town. The drive was
an eight-hour ordeal, and I used my car and paid for the
gas simply because she asked.) I let people stay at my house
for as long as they liked, and listened to the problems of
others for two, three and even four hours at a time. This
need to be needed by others was very empowering and I
felt useful, but at the same time it was very disempowering
because I constantly felt used and unappreciated.

Today I do not lend more than a dollar, allow people to
stay at my house for long periods of time, do other people's
laundry, lend my valuable material possessions to
strangers or bake cookies for the entire recovering community in my area. Also I do not spend hours on the
phone listening to the problems of others. I started setting
limits with myself, boundaries with others and learned
that I had to come first in my own recovery process.

Most of us look outside ourselves for that "fix" which will make us feel complete because we feel so empty and alone on the inside. We use alcohol, drugs, food, work, sex, relationships, power, money, status, material possessions and more in an attempt to fill ourselves up. Addiction for many of us becomes the parenting we never had. Initially we feel safe and protected, but eventually it becomes a monster that causes us shame and pain.

Many of us were disempowered as children by being told our feelings were wrong, as were our perceptions. We were led to believe all adults were always right. We were empowered as a result of being forced to grow up too fast with praises for "not getting dirty," for "being quiet" and for "being big girls and boys." The praise felt good but the price that was paid out for this approval was the loss of our childhood.

Children have a right to be children, and children have a right to be vulnerable, imperfect and curious. Only in this way can children grow into healthy adults who know how to take care of themselves responsibly in the world. For those of us who have missed out on some of the growth childhood provides, it is necessary to give ourselves permission to return to our childhood to learn the valuable lessons childhood teaches.

Effects Of Childhood Emotional Abuse On Developing Boundaries

2

Emotional Abuse

We live in a society where many forms of abuse are an accepted way of life. We do not prepare new parents with guidelines for raising healthy children. New parents, as a consequence of the lack of attention given to healthy parenting skills, are often left with only two choices with regard to parenting their own children: as they were parented themselves or the complete opposite of how they were parented. If our parents parented us in unhealthy ways, our parenting of our children will be dysfunctional, even when our style of parenting is completely opposite. We are a society of extremes. We will either disempower our children with rigid rules and shaming abuse, or we will overempower them by not setting limits or providing healthy guidelines.

As my son, Aaron, grew through his toddler years, he continued to explore his world and experiment with setting limits. He would attempt to work me against my husband or vice versa when trying to push limits. Children naturally push to see how far they can go.

Bubble gum became a big issue in our household for quite some time. Aaron would go to his father, asking for bubble gum. If Dad said no, Aaron would then come to me with the same request. If Michael and I were not communicating with one another, chances are I would unknowingly sabotage Michael's position of father by giving Aaron bubble gum instead of talking about it with Michael first. If a child cannot get what he or she needs or wants from one parent, the child will go to the other parent with the same request. This is natural normal childhood behavior.

Children "pit" one parent against another, attempting to get what they want. Unfortunately, in many situations, parents will use this process to fulfill their needs when these needs are not being met in the marital relationship. If a married couple are not addressing the conflicts within their relationship, resolution of marital difficulty is impossible. Many couples have difficulty expressing their anger towards one another in healthy ways. As a consequence the children may be brought in as a vehicle for expressing this anger. The scenario for such a situation might appear as follows:

JERRY'S STORY | Dad is a nonrecovering workaholic and an adult child of an alcoholic, who is rarely at home. He fears addressing his own unfinished business, which is spilling over into his marital relationship with his wife. His wife is also a nonrecovering adult child of an alcoholic who has a great deal of difficulty expressing her anger. She feels lonely and frustrated because her husband is rarely home to help her with her two sons. When her husband is at home, she feels he is still emotionally unavailable because he is so distracted with his many home improvement projects.

In despair, she often shares her frustration about her husband's lack of attention to the family with Jerry, her oldest (13-year-old) son. She also expects Jerry to be the "man of the house" in his father's absence and help care for his younger brother. Jerry's mother constantly tells him how important it is for him to be strong and that she really depends on him. There are even times when Jerry's mother comes to him in tears over disagreements between her and his father. Jerry feels uncomfortable listening to his mother cry and often wishes his father would do something about it. Jerry feels angry with both of his parents for not solving their problems with one another and he feels trapped.

Jerry and his friends decide to go to the movies one Friday night, then have burgers on the way home. Jerry goes to his father to ask for some money for his Friday evening out. His father gives him five dollars and tells him this amount should cover his expenses. Jerry asks his father for more, hoping to get a few more bucks for some candy, and his father says no.

His mother, hearing all of this, pulls Jerry aside and slips him five more dollars. Jerry knows his mother would give him what he wanted without any struggle because he knows he can always get what he wants from her. Jerry also knows that the best time to ask mother for something is when she is upset with his father. Jerry asks his mother if he can stay out past his curfew. And, as Jerry predicted, she says yes. Jerry has a great time with the guys and upon returning home notices his father is still up. His father tells him he has broken curfew and will be grounded for the next week. Jerry tells his father that his mother gave him permission to stay out late. Jerry's father tells him he did not clear this change of plan with him and that he will still be punished. Jerry is angry with his father but knows this punishment will be "fixed" by his mother.

This child is being severely abused by both parents, and his chance to learn about healthy boundaries is very limited. In this situation Jerry's mother, lonely and frustrated with his father, has elevated him from the role of child to one of surrogate spouse. She has empowered him and set him up to believe it is his job to take care of her. She has also overempowered him by sabotaging his father's attempts at disciplining. This places Jerry in a position of power over his father.

Jerry is learning it is his job to take care of women and that his payoff for doing so will be to "get what he wants" from them. Although the power Jerry is given by his mother may feel affirming, it is at the same time very abusive. Jerry is losing out by not being allowed his role of child. He will also grow up having difficulty in relationships with females because he will want to be in control and caretake. This will sabotage true intimacy in a relationship as he will always see himself in a one-up position with women. He will attract women who are in need of caretaking as a consequence of addiction and their own unfinished business. Jerry will not attract or be able to have a healthy relationship with a self-sufficient, healthy woman.

Fearful and unresolved about his own life, Jerry's father has also emotionally abused his son. He is just as responsible for setting up Jerry's role as surrogate spouse as his wife is. Jerry's father abandoned Jerry and left him to take care of his wife so that he would not have to deal with her. He also set his older son up to be father to his younger son. He, too, forced his older boy to grow up too fast. Jerry's father taught him to not ask for help and to just avoid conflict. Jerry's father did not model those tools necessary for problem-solving in healthy ways. He set him up to avoid conflict and painful feelings by distracting. He also did not model healthy communication skills and, as a result, Jerry will have great difficulty communicating in adulthood.

Jerry will run from problems and never think about asking for help. He will have difficulty knowing how to problem-solve, which will interfere with his ability to have healthy intimacy with others. Healthy intimacy involves conflict resolution and if we are lacking in those tools, life problems are rarely resolved and usually avoided. Jerry also will have difficulty having healthy relationships with men. Our relationship with our same-sexed parent sets the stage for our relationships with same-sexed peers. If we do not have a healthy relationship with our same-sexed parent, we will not know how to trust and interact in healthy ways with those of the same sex as us.

Triangulation

Both of Jerry's parents used him as the "go-between" for their anger with one another. This is called *triangulation*. Jerry's mother and father need to talk with one another about their marital problems. Instead, Mom talks with Jerry about her problems with his father. This angers Jerry's father so he gets back at his wife by abandoning his son and using harsh discipline. Jerry's mother retaliates by sabotaging her husband's authority and rescuing her son from his father.

As we can clearly see, Jerry's needs as a 13-year-old child are not foremost in the minds of his parents. He is a Ping-Pong ball between his parents who are not direct with one another about their feelings. Jerry's boundaries are not being respected or nurtured by his parents as they are both using him.

Jerry will have difficulty in adulthood during times of conflict, especially when the conflict is between two people. He will find himself involved over and over again in the conflicts of others, be they two friends, two relatives or two colleagues on the job. Having grown up believing it was his responsibility to solve his parents' problems, he will continue this pattern in other relationships. Jerry will rescue people from conflict and interfere with their process of resolution. He will get "sucked into" arguments between others and be expected to choose sides. Jerry will constantly feel used, confused, frustrated and trapped — never knowing how he becomes involved in one dysfunctional situation after another.

Jerry's abuse from his family of origin is emotional abuse, which can be as devastating as physical or sexual abuse. Many of us have been emotionally abused but are unaware of it. Some of us are emotionally abusive to our own children, not seeing how painful our own words can really be.

Unhealthy Situation

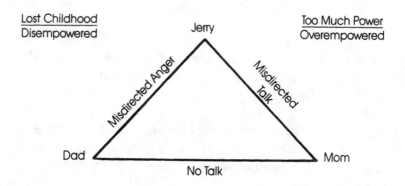

Healthy Situation

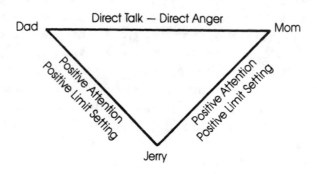

Allowed Childhood
Not Involved In Adult Disputes

Figure 2.1. Examples Of Triangulation

Emotional abuse takes on many forms, and for our purposes we will examine those which are most obvious.

Some forms of emotional abuse are direct, hurtful statements used to disempower and shame the victim into submission. Many of us have been called degrading names, such as stupid, ingrate, dumb blond, crybaby, dumb ass, slut, bad boy, whore, moron, pansy and more. It is emotionally abusive to call a child names which are degrading or which are labeling in a demeaning way.

SARAH'S STORY | Sarah's father was an angry, violent alcoholic. He would go to the bars at night and drink until closing time. When he finally came home from the bars, he would either pass out on the living room floor or wake up the household with complaints about chores not being completed. Sarah was a 15-year-old, shy girl who made very good grades, had just started dating a few of the boys at school and was well liked. She did her chores when she came home from school and helped her mother with her two younger brothers.

Sarah felt sorry for her mother and wished she would divorce her father. She couldn't understand why her mother put up with his abusive behavior. Sometimes if Sarah's father was really drunk, he would come home from the bar and lecture her about boys. He would call her a slut and tell her he knew she was not a "good girl." Sarah was terrified of sex and couldn't understand why her father was accusing her of such things. He would shame her about how she dressed, telling her good girls did not wear jeans or makeup. Sarah became very confused because all of her friends wore jeans and makeup to school and were not being accused of appearing "loose" or "easy" by their parents. Sarah's father believed there were only two types of women, prostitutes and good girls. Sarah tried really hard to be a "good girl" and couldn't understand why her father thought she was a "bad girl."

Denigrating Labels

Sarah will have a difficult time feeling comfortable with her own sexuality. She will have constant concerns about appearing to be too easy or loose and have difficulty experimenting with her femininity. Her first experience of an intimate relationship with a man was in her relationship with her father. Sarah may generalize and believe all men are like her father, seeing women as either "prostitutes" or "madonnas." Since her father disempowered her by calling her a slut, chances are she will be attracted to men who disempower and degrade her. Since she will not trust men and has a low sense of self-worth, she will feel uncomfortable and not trust men who treat her with respect and kindness.

In some situations, children literally take on the labels they have been given in childhood. Sarah, for instance, may decide, "Since my father constantly accuses me of being a slut, I might as well go find out what it feels like to have sex." Sarah may begin a series of sexual relationships, hoping this will fill up the loss she carries within. If she allows herself to be used sexually by others, the pattern of disempowerment continues. She may also discover by sexually acting out, she feels empowered and that sex gives her a false sense of control over men. The acting-out behavior temporarily covers up the degradation and feelings of disempowerment which come from being abused and used by her father and other men. But eventually the feelings of shame and sense of being used returns.

Name-calling can be life-damaging, and the consequences can affect all areas of our lives. It is important to examine those names we have been called in our youth to determine if they continue to impact us today. I am six feet tall and was called "Jolly Green Giant." I do not believe it was done out of maliciousness, but it did affect my sense of self as a tall person. I felt unhappy about being tall and was ashamed of my height. I slumped and refused to wear high heels for quite some time. The statement "Jolly Green Giant" was disempowering and set me up to feel "less than" for being tall. I felt I wasn't good enough or as acceptable as shorter people.

It is also abusive to call children Mama's big boy, Daddy's little princess, Mama's little man, Daddy's sweetheart or Mommy's special one too frequently. These statements are cute and on the outside appear to be harmless, but the meanings of these phrases carry a powerful punch for children. Spoken periodically they can be affirming and special but, verbalized excessively, they become labels that affect a small child's developing concept of self. When children are labeled with phrases such as these, they are being disempowered and, in many cases, overempowered at the same time.

With 13-year-old Jerry, we remember what weight and responsibility "Mama's little man of the house" carried for this young boy. He was empowered with the label, "little man," and given authority and power over his younger brother. Jerry was placed in the role of surrogate father and husband in his father's absence. The power and sense of being "more grown up" than 13 temporarily felt good, but the sad consequence of this role was the loss of his childhood. It is difficult to feel comfortable being a vulnerable immature child who makes mistakes when thrust into the role of a tiny adult.

Some of us come from families where the demand for perfection was overwhelming. We heard statements like "What will the neighbors think . . . Always put your best foot forward . . . If you don't succeed at first try, try again . . . You have opportunities I never had, so use them all . . . Stand up straight . . . Don't put your elbows on the table . . . If you can't say anything nice, don't say anything at all . . . Children are to be seen and not heard," and the list goes on. To demand perfection from naturally immature imperfect children is emotionally abusive, and it can stunt experimentation and creativity. Children learn about boundaries and the world around them by making mistakes and creative experimenting.

Also statements such as "Quit crying like a baby" or "If you're going to act like that, leave the room" and "Nice girls don't get angry" sabotage a child's ability to learn and heal from life's pain and frustration. Most of us have difficulty healing from the pain life brings because we feel uncomfortable with our feelings of frustration, anger and sadness. We feel insecure with such feelings, fearing our vulnerability will be discovered. Most of us as children were rarely given permission to be vulnerable.

It is emotionally abusive not to allow a child to express his or her feelings. My son, Aaron, would periodically have angry tantrums. This is normal child behavior. When he would have a tantrum, it was acceptable for him to pound his feet, cry and even verbalize with whom or why he was angry at the top of his lungs. My job as a parent was to let him be angry. When we allow our children their feelings, it is also important to set limits at the same time. So when Aaron would have a tantrum, it was not acceptable for him to hit or kick another person or throw things across the room. Children also need to know that while they are experiencing intense feelings, there will be an adult around who will set limits for them. This gives them a sense of security. How many of us were allowed to be spontaneous feeling children, while at the same time were given healthy guidelines for experiencing our feelings in safety?

The Silent Treatment

Some of us were disciplined with "the silent treatment." The silent treatment involves being abandoned, avoided, not talked to, banished or ignored when a child's behavior does not meet the approval of parents or other adults. The silent treatment is a powerful technique which has been used by many adults as a method of control and discipline for children for many generations. The thought usually is, "Well, it's better than hitting children." In reality this method of control is just as harmful as physical abuse.

Children have shared with me that they would rather have a spanking as a punishment than the silent treatment. Children can numb out during a spanking, which is usually done quickly. It is difficult to numb out during the silent treatment so the emotional pain hurts much longer. The silent treatment nonverbally says to a child, "If you make a mistake and are not perfect, I will ignore you as if you do not exist." This sets children up to grow into adults who either have an insatiable need to be heard and may be very self-centered, or they may become adults who fear sharing an idea because of an overwhelming fear of being abandoned for having a differing opinion.

A number of us grew up in homes where one or both of our parents would rage at us or one another. There is a big difference between feeling healthy anger and abusive rage. Anger is healthy and it gives us the power we need to take those actions necessary to care for and protect ourselves. In healthy families all members are allowed to have feelings of anger. Anger allows families to "blow out the pipes" and resolve conflict. It brings families closer together because communication is opened up.

Rageaholism

Rage is the stuffed feeling of anger which suddenly blows up uncontrollably and is used to control, scare and intimidate others into submission. Usually in dysfunctional families only one or two people in the family are allowed to rage. Other family members are not even allowed the feelings or expression of healthy anger. To be raged at or exposed to the raging behavior of another is very abusive. When a child is raged at, they learn very quickly to shut down in order to protect themselves. Shutting down means to numb out or disassociate, being completely void of feeling.

I am a recovering rageaholic and grew up with parents who raged at each other, myself and my younger sisters. When one of my parents would rage, I would go into a daydream or fantasy in order to avoid the feelings of pain and terror I had about their raging. As an adult I had great difficulty expressing my anger in healthy ways. I would constantly allow myself to be abused by others and drift into numbness or fantasy to avoid the pain.

Occasionally instead of numbing out, I would insulate myself with walls of rage to push people away and protect myself from pain. I would swing from having absolutely no boundaries or protection at all to building isolating, intimidating walls of rage. When I would rage, those around me were confused, emotionally abused and fearful.

I was doing to others what had been done to me, continuing the cycle of emotionally abusive unhealthy behavior.

Healthy anger is neither intimidating nor fear-inducing. I had to learn how to have my angry feelings as they occurred, instead of stuffing them until I raged uncontrollably. I also had to learn how to be more aware of when I was being used or abused, instead of drifting off into a fantasy to avoid the pain. Once I became aware of when I was being used, abused, discounted or shamed, I was able to begin taking the action necessary to protect and care for myself in healthy ways. I no longer had to swing from being victimized to isolating and emotionally hurting others. We must all learn how to be responsible for ourselves and this awareness only comes as we begin exploring how we grew up.

Children begin learning about healthy expression of feelings at a very early age. They watch and absorb everything and truly believe all adults are right at all times. Imagine how confusing it would be for a child to grow up with a parent who rages and then tells the child he or she cannot express their own feelings of anger.

Many adults stuff their anger and give their children a double message. Children feel everything but usually don't know why they are feeling the way they do. I see many young children who are experiencing difficulty at home or in school. They are having problems sleeping, their grades fluctuate or drop, they are fighting with siblings or friends. There is a feeling of generalized discontent. When I ask them how they are feeling, they may say sad, mad or scared, but when I ask them why they are feeling this way, they respond with, "I don't know." They truly don't know because in many cases they are acting out those feelings their parents are not addressing and resolving. Because of this, I always insist upon seeing both parents with the child. Usually the parents have a lot of unfinished business and unresolved conflict which they need to address. Interestingly, as they address their own issues, their children's behavior improves.

SALLY'S STORY | Many parents fear expressing their anger in front of their children so their children grow up feeling confused about their own feelings of anger. Sally was raised with two parents who feared being "bad parents." Her parents worked very hard at providing her with the material and emotional needs necessary for her development, working very hard to provide a healthy environment for both Sally and her brother to grow up in. They always put their children first. Sally's parents never argued in front of her. She knew when they were angry, but never saw them fight. She would even ask her mother during these times, "Are you and Daddy mad at each other?" And her mother would say, "Of course not!"

When Sally grew up she began having relationships which never seemed to last. Each time there was conflict or disagreement, Sally would end the relationship. Sally was very depressed as she shared the ending of another relationship with her mother. Her mother responded, "I can't understand why you are having such a difficult time. Your father and I never fought in front of you or your brother." And Sally replied, "Since you never fought in front of me, I don't know how to argue or resolve disagreement. I never learned how to deal with conflict."

Spiritual Abuse

Some of us grew up in homes where religion played a very important part in our development. Spiritual guidance gives children a foundation for learning from the hardships of life. A spiritual foundation provides us with a philosophy to understand loss and pain. A healthy spiritual background gives us guidelines and inner resources. Some of us were not given a healthy spiritual philosophy during childhood, which is spiritually abusive.

Our first concept of a Higher Power comes from our family of origin. Our parents pass on to us their beliefs, values and traditions regarding religion. The adults we grow up with also provide a base for our understanding of a Higher Power or God. If our parents are critical, rigid or abusive, we will have a concept of a Higher Power which is critical, rigid or abusive. If our parents were supportive, nurturing and safe, we will have beliefs in a supportive, nurturing and safe Higher Power. I have not met one atheist yet who was not a victim of some type of childhood abuse. As one atheist put it, "How can I believe in a God that cares for me when my family was so sick? If there was a God, why did I have to get so abused?"

GEORGE'S STORY   In some situations children swing completely counter to their parents in their spiritual beliefs. George was raised by two alcoholic parents, both of whom physically abused him. George never really understood why his parents behaved the way they did and while growing up, he wished he was in another family. In junior high he became very involved in a teenage church program with a friend of his. When at church, he felt safe and loved. George always knew he could escape the hardships of home by going to church. At church everybody treated him as a family member so that the closeness among his church friends gave him a sense of security. George remained in this church throughout his teen years and on into adulthood.

The church told him he needed to forgive his parents and move on with his life. Although George thought he had forgiven his parents, he continued on occasion to feel empty inside. Periodically he would be overwhelmed with feelings of intense rage and sadness. George became even more involved in the church, hoping that by helping others these feelings would go away.

Eventually George married a woman from his church and together they produced a son named Doug. George and his wife wanted Doug to have a strong church upbringing and started to involve him in church activities at a very early age. George read to his son out of the Bible on a regular basis and the beliefs and principles of the church were discussed daily.

When Doug was nine years old, his father caught him smoking cigarettes behind the house. George spanked Doug with the belt and told him he was not following the ways of the church. George read to his son from the Bible and told Doug that God was very angry with him for smoking cigarettes. Doug was confused and hurt with his father's reaction. He was just messing around and trying to see what was so great about cigarettes. A lot of people at church smoked and he just wanted to try it. He knew he would be punished somehow for smoking, but he didn't expect what he received. He was also confused about God and began fearing God really was angry with him and that God was going to punish him, too.

When Doug was 13, one of his friends offered him a puff off a marijuana cigarette. Doug had been smoking tobacco cigarettes since he was nine and decided to try this new cigarette. His father had told him that all drug users were sinners who went to hell, but Doug knew his father thought everybody outside of the church was a sinner destined for doom in the hereafter. He also felt his father thought of him as a sinner already so that it no longer mattered if he took a smoke of marijuana.

One day Doug's mother was putting away the family laundry and found some pills in Doug's dresser drawer. She immediately told her husband about her discovery. Neither of them could understand where they had gone wrong with their son. George had promised himself that he would be the parent *his* parents never were and was confused and hurt when he realized his son was into drugs.

George had never healed from the abuse he had suffered as a consequence of growing up in a violent alcoholic family. He had found refuge in the church from his pain and discovered the church provided him with the nurturing he so desperately needed. Though the church provided some safety and security for George, it did not heal him from his pain about being abused. The church had provided a temporary bandage for his pain, but George needed to experience his feelings about his childhood in order to heal the emptiness within. George had hoped the church would be the answer to growing up with alcoholic parents, but unfortunately he was in need of more help than the church could provide.

At the time George had needed guidelines to live by because his parents were unable to provide them because of their addiction to alcohol. The church gave George the surrogate parenting he so desperately needed, but not resolutions of the feelings he still carried about the physical and emotional abuse he endured in his youth.

George and his wife had expected that their son, Doug, would follow the ways of the church. But instead Doug rebelled, not against the church, but against his parents' rigidity. The survival skills George acquired while growing up with alcoholic parents were passed on to Doug, who, like his father, was looking for acceptance and healthy guidance. Doug's father and mother were religious addicts who were addicted to the high of self-righteousness. By believing their way of living was the only way, they had insulated themselves from the realities of life and were unable to provide their son, Doug, with the healthy tools necessary for living in the real world.

Teenage Separating

Part of growing up during adolescence involves separating from our parents by rebelling. Teenagers begin testing themselves and their environment by questioning their parents' belief systems. This is healthy in that it prepares the teenager for leaving the safety of the family to venture into the real world. Teenagers experiment with their identity in order to begin discovering who they are. In a healthy family they know intuitively that if they move too quickly or too soon through this process, their parents will still be available to set limits for them by providing guidance, safety and discipline. When parents are too rigid, teens are not able to begin the process of separation in a healthy manner. They either stay enmeshed with the family — never to discover who they really are — or they totally rebel and completely reject what their parents stand for.

In Doug's case he was genetically predisposed to the disease of chemical addiction because his grandparents were alcoholic. He also rebelled against his parents' values and beliefs because the rigidity within his family system was so overwhelming. It was difficult for him to embrace his father's concept of God because his father had constantly told Doug God was angry with his behavior.

Religious Manipulation

Whenever a child is punished or threatened with the · wrath of God or "God doesn't approve" or "You're a sinner" or "God is watching and upset," this is spiritually abusive. Children literally believe what their parents tell them and if a parent tells a child, "God doesn't like you," they truly believe God is angry with them and in some cases fear punishment.

It is also not appropriate to use the Bible as a weapon for disciplining children. When parents use religious principles to shame, threaten or punish their children, this sets religion up to be a scary, fearful authoritarian institution. A parent's rigid religious beliefs can sabotage the development of healthy spirituality. Religion is an institution which can help us understand our own spirituality, but when it is abusive or used to control others, it is no longer serving the spiritual development of those involved in the religion.

Spiritual abuse during childhood can affect our ability to explore ourselves as spiritual beings in adulthood. It is important for us to look at our family of origin's religious beliefs to determine whether or not they are in any way stunting our own spiritual growth. Also whenever an adult, be it a parent, relative, pastor, teacher or any other grown person, abuses a child physically, emotionally or sexually, they are also abusing the child's spirituality. A child's first concept of a Higher Power has the characteristics of those adults living in the child's environment. If a child is abused by an adult, the child's concept of a Higher Power will be one of a punishing, abusive Higher Power who is to be feared.

Hopefully we will all discover our true spiritual selves as we continue to explore who we are and where we come from. By discovering our spiritual selves, we raise our self-esteem and begin to realize we are worth taking care of. We become our own best friend, realizing we do not have to be victims of the world or isolate ourselves from the life experience.

We need to examine those nonverbal and verbal messages we received in childhood which are still affecting us today. A number of us were directly assaulted with hurtful words that cut deeply into our very souls and we need to heal from these wounds. Others still carry within those labels received from their parents and continue to act them out and give them life in adulthood. For most of us, our parents' intent with these messages was not to abuse or hurt, but unfortunately we still carry the scars of the pain they inflicted.

It is important for our growth to re-examine what was said to us and heal from those statements that hurt and wounded our concepts of self. When we heal from our pain about what was said to us, we are free to let go of these labels and phrases and are no longer ruled by their meanings. As they lose their power, we can finally begin to explore who we really are.

Physical And Sexual Abuse On Developing Boundaries | 3

Physical Abuse

Many times people will share with me how they were disciplined with the belt. When I say to them, "That was physically abusive," their response is, "Oh, no. That's just how I was disciplined."

The issue of paddling children in our school systems continues to raise controversies. Many of us were disciplined with spankings because this is how our parents were disciplined by *their* elders. It is often difficult to explain to people who were disciplined in this way that they have been abused. This form of discipline is also a result of the lack of healthy options parents have for setting limits with their children. When a parent hits a child with a belt, coat hanger, tree limb, hairbrush or other implement, it is difficult to tell how hard the blows really are. If I hit the table top with my hand, my hand reacts with pain, and I can gauge the force with which I wish to hit. If I hit the table top with a brush or coat hanger, it is difficult to know just how hard I am hitting. In a rage a parent can cause a great deal of injury to a child when hitting with an implement because they are totally unaware of how hard they are hitting the child.

I am not an advocate of spanking in any form. Hitting does not teach; it intimidates. When spanking is used as a form of discipline, the child defocuses off the reason for the discipline and focuses in on being hit, to do what is necessary to avoid the physical pain, be that numbing out physically or going into a fantasy.

When children are hit they learn that hitting is an acceptable behavior, and they may begin hitting their sibling or friends at school. When children are spanked, they are no longer able to learn healthy boundaries. The message of physical abuse is, "I am bigger and more powerful, and I will hurt you if you make a mistake or do not meet my standards." Some children become so far removed from why they are being punished that awareness of what they have done to deserve discipline is lost.

JULIE'S STORY | In adulthood, the consequences of childhood hitting are acted out in several different ways. Julie's father abandoned her and her mother when she was two years old. Her mother never healed from her loss, and for many years would pace the floor at night awaiting her husband's return. She also worked two jobs to support herself and her daughter, often feeling overwhelmed with the responsibility of being a single parent. She felt inadequate as a parent and periodically would blow up and hit her daughter when she felt out of control and trapped. Julie could never understand why her mother was always so angry with her, no matter how good she was.

Julie grew up and married John, who was an alcoholic and emotionally distant. She consistently felt abandoned by John and would rage and shame him about his drinking. John would stop drinking for short periods of time, but eventually would start up again. One day Julie became so infuriated with her situation that she lost all control and smashed pieces of her best china. She felt much shame about her behavior and wondered whether she just couldn't leave her husband and take care of herself.

Julie had been victimized by her mother's physical and emotional raging behavior and had also been abandoned by her father. These old wounds were never healed, and Julie continued to recreate the environment in which she grew up in her adult life. We are drawn to what is familiar and live our lives by the rules and traditions we grew up with. They may not be the exact same rules, but they are incredibly similar. Julie never learned how to have healthy anger in childhood, and her only model for the expression of angry feelings was her mother. Julie reacts to her current life situation in the same way her mother reacted when she felt alone and overwhelmed.

Some of us are so fearful of becoming like our parents, we react 180 degrees in the opposite direction. The only physical contacts John ever received while growing up were spankings. He was rarely hugged and never kissed. John's father was a very angry man but he would never verbally express it. Everybody in John's family knew when their father was angry and would react by slinking up to their rooms. Usually when John's father was angry, someone in the family would be disciplined.

When his father would discipline John, he would have him first go to the backyard and get a limb from the peach tree. Then after all of the leaves had been stripped off, John would be switched. John was not allowed to cry because his father would hit him even more if he saw tears. John would numb his body and hold his breath. He would desperately try not to cry out to show his father just how tough he was.

When John first witnessed Julie in a rage, he felt scared and didn't know what to do. For several years John had noticed that he had a difficult time with angry people. When somebody was angry, he just wanted to disappear. When Julie was angry with him, he wanted to fade away. John learned how to ignore Julie's raging, and on many occasions would leave the house during such times, going into the garage with a couple of beers. John found that beer helped him relax and took the edge off his nerves.

When we experience pain, our natural tendency is to cry. Crying provides a release for the pain we feel and allows us to heal emotionally.

When a child is told not to cry while being physically abused, they are being told to not listen to their bodies, not to trust their bodies. They learn to distrust their feelings in order to survive the pain they are experiencing.

John learned how to survive emotional and physical trauma by tuning out, and he learned how to avoid conflict with alcohol.

During childhood if we are raised in dysfunctional families, we develop a specific set of survival skills to allow us to live with the dysfunction. These skills keep us safe and allow us to make sense out of our unhealthy environments. We take these survival skills with us into adulthood and eventually notice they do not work in the here and now. They fit in our family of origin because they were tailored for that specific environment, but in our adult experiences they seem outdated. Recovery is about examining our survival skills in order to determine whether or not they still fit our needs in adulthood.

SANDY'S | Sandy grew up in a family that looked like the
STORY | perfect All-American Family. She had an older sister and a younger brother. Her father worked hard at the office all day and her mother stayed at home with her, her sister and her brother. Both of her parents were very involved with the church and went several times during the week. Sandy's father was a lay pastor at their church and her mother was a Sunday school teacher. Sometimes Sandy would become annoyed at the amount of time spent at church. All of her school friends were riding their bikes and going to slumber parties while she had to be in church. Sandy's parents encouraged her to associate only with those children in the church and never allowed her to go to slumber parties with her school friends. She felt left out and isolated and really wanted to feel a part of her

friends at school. She would make up excuses why she could not join them, fearful they would find out the truth.

After school some of her friends would go and get sodas. They always invited her to join in but she had to make up excuses because she didn't have the money for sodas.

Her father used to put his spare change on the breakfast table when he came home from the office. One day Sandy decided to take a couple of coins to pay for soda. She went out with her friends and really enjoyed herself, so she took a few more coins the next day. That evening her father found out and told her he would have to punish her: She was only allowed bread and milk for her meals for a week. She was also not allowed to associate with her schoolmates.

In adulthood Sandy had trouble feeling comfortable with people and never felt that she fit in. She had difficulty in relationships. The men she became involved with always seemed so controlling. It was as if they wanted to own her. They would tell her what to wear and how to act. She was frustrated because she felt as if she didn't really know who she was and that nobody in her life was willing to let her find out. Her parents called several times a week, and she felt overwhelmed with their constant concern for her. She was 28 years old and still felt as if she were five years old when she talked with them. She wished they would give her some space and let her grow up.

Sandy's parents were religious addicts who wanted to isolate their child from the real world. But if we do not have contact with, or are overprotected from, school friends and life experiences, we will not develop the tools necessary for surviving safely in the real world.

When a parent shares concerns with me about who their children are associating with, they usually share in the same breath that they have restricted their child from visiting with certain peers. Usually the reasoning behind these restrictions have to do with race, religion, politics or social stature of the parents. In many situations when children are told not to associate with a certain peer, this only intensifies their desire for the relationship. It is physically abusive to isolate a child from his or her peers. If a peer has behaviors that are undesirable, it is important for parents to provide healthy guidelines and tools to help a child reach a conclusion about whether or not this peer will be a good friend. If a child experiences difficulty because of an undesirable peer, this experience will be the best teacher. Children learn about friendship by interacting with their peers. With healthy support from parents they can then develop the tools necessary for experiencing healthy safe relationships in adulthood with all types of people. To push a child into isolation, or relationships with only certain types of people, cheats them out of learning how to develop boundaries, work with others and experience healthy intimacy.

Sandy's father also abused her with his punishment of bread and milk for a week. Depriving a child of food, clothing, shelter, medical attention or healthy physical touch is physically abusive. Many of us have come from families where we were not beaten but were not given healthy physical touch or nurturing. Everybody needs healthy physical touch and everybody needs food, clothing, shelter and medical attention. These are basic physical needs.

If we do not have these needs taken care of during childhood, many of us grow up into adults who do not know how to eat healthy foods, dress ourselves appropriately, protect ourselves or take ourselves to the doctor when we are ill. Parents teach children how to take care of their basic needs by caring for these needs in childhood. When a parent does not take care of these needs, the message the child receives is, I am not worthwhile enough to be taken care of. This message continues in adulthood and needy adults can't take care of themselves.

My parents divorced when I was 11 years old, and my two sisters and I lived with my mother. My mother was an overwhelmed single parent who consoled herself with alcohol and prescription medication. She worked two jobs and was rarely available emotionally. When she was home, she was under the influence of alcohol or prescription medication or both, so we knew not to bother mother.

She had grown up with parents who isolated her from all painful experiences. They smothered and overprotected her. She was the center of their life, and they gave to her materially and emotionally in excess. She never learned how to take care of herself and survive effectively in the adult world. Because she did not know how to take care of herself, she had difficulty caring for my sisters and me. Mother would only take us to the doctor or dentist if somebody else told her to do so or if a medical problem was obvious. My mother had very few skills for dealing with us when we were sick.

I remember my grandmother would come to the house when one of us was really ill, and the first thing she would do would be to tell my mother to leave the room. When I grew up, I had great difficulty allowing myself to be sick. Grandmother had over-reacted to illness, and my mother had under-reacted. When feeling under the weather, I would fluctuate from believing I had a terminal illness to not caring for myself at all.

Having healthy boundaries involves knowing how to care for self and protecting our bodies in healthy ways. Many of us are constantly at the doctor's office, worried about every little scrape and bump while others haven't seen a doctor or dentist in years. Recovery and developing healthy boundaries is about learning how not to live in the extremes. Many of us today have to learn the proper ways to eat, sleep and dress ourselves. We also have to deal with our feelings about having to learn these basic tasks in adulthood.

Learning To Have Fun

Another activity we are supposed to learn, along with taking care of our basic needs, is how to have fun. Fun is an important part of childhood because it teaches us that life is supposed to be enjoyable. Most parents and children enjoy rough-housing, rolling on the floor, tickling and chasing each other around the house. These activities are delightful for child and parent alike. It allows child and parent to play with one another and children learn that it's acceptable to be playful in adulthood. These activities teach the importance of spontaneity and play.

In some play situations parents become too rough and tickling is done in excess. It is fun until it becomes too rough. Children learn about setting boundaries by saying stop or no to physical touch and having the requests respected. Some children are tickled until they wet their pants while others receive physical injury as a consequence of rough-housing with a parent. When a child says stop or no to physical touch, and tickling or rough-housing continues, this is no longer play. Play becomes physically abusive, and children learn they haven't any rights to their bodies and that their needs are not important. Usually parents haven't any idea that they are physically abusing their children during these times because they see this behavior as play.

It is important for children to experience healthy physical touch so that they can develop a healthy sense of confidence in self. When our bodies are violated as a consequence of physical abuse, we are at risk for allowing others to abuse us emotionally or physically in adulthood or we may become just like the abuser we feared in childhood. It is also important to be provided with opportunities in childhood which require an element of risk in relationships with others and with childhood experiences. With guidelines and healthy protection from parents, children can begin to learn about the uncertainties of the real world in the safety of their homes. If we are not allowed to risk in childhood, we are cheated out of those experiences which prepare us for healthy adulthood. We feel at a loss and learn to isolate ourselves from the world in which we live.

Sexual Abuse

Recently the issue of sexual abuse has been receiving more attention and it appears as though it is on the rise. In reality what is really happening is that sexual abuse is finally coming out of the closet as more sexual abuse survivors break the "no-talk rule" and share their experience, strength and hope with the general population. Also more helping professionals are able to recognize better the symptoms of a sexual abuse survivor and effectively address the trauma of sexual abuse. Most sexual abuse survivors have no memory of their abuse, but they may have several of the following symptoms as a consequence of such trauma.

Disassociation: Difficulty feeling connected with others. Difficulty feeling a part of life.

Out-of-body experiences: Feeling at times in adulthood or childhood that one has been outside of the physical body. In some instances sexual abuse survivors share feelings about being above their physical body looking down or across the room observing.

Excessive fantasy: Drifting off into a daydream excessively. Living in an emotional fantasy or seeking fantasy excessively through books, television, movies.

Inappropriate reactions: Out of touch with feelings or over-reacting with feelings. Not knowing how to cry or have anger at appropriate times. Over-reacting to situations outside of self, such as television commercials, with excessive tears, rage or fear.

Not noticing physical pain: Out of touch with the body's need for food, rest or healthy touch. Not noticing or feeling physical pain during or after an injury has occurred.

Phobias, overwhelming fears: Excessive fear of crowds, flying, doctors, dentists, shots, animals, dirt or germs. Excessive fear of certain types of people, places or things.

Panic attacks, anxiety attacks (consequences of feeling out of control): Hyperventilating or difficulty breathing, upset stomach or feeling as though one is going to vomit, wanting to hide and isolate, feeling dizzy, hot or as though one is going to pass out.

Distorted perception of physical, emotional or social self: Unrealistic perception of the physical body. Intense dislike of the physical body. Viewing self as emotionally superior or inferior to others to the point of feeling separate from others. Feeling socially inadequate in social situations. Isolating from others or having little involvement with others. Feeling socially superior with a need to be in control of others at all times. Having an overwhelming need for power.

Inappropriate boundaries: Not knowing how to protect self. Feeling constantly used, abused or victimized by others. Not knowing how to say no to others or set limits with family, friends or in job situations. Overly trusting or the "open-book syndrome." Fearful of authority. Feeling frozen, numb or frightened when confronted. Not knowing how to defend self. Hiding behind walls of rage, fear or shame to isolate and avoid others. Offending others when feeling threatened and at risk. Fearful of being exposed or hurt and presenting a false front of security. An overwhelming fear of being out of control. Intense lack of trust, overly cautious and suspicious of others and their motives.

Self-destructive behavior: Suicidal tendencies involving attempting, planning or following through with self-destructive acts. Allowing others to physically, emotionally or sexually abuse self. Picking on scabs or wounds. Chewing nails and pulling out hair. Cutting oneself with razor blades or purposefully doing things to the physical body which inflict pain. Sadomasochistic or sadistic behavior.

Destructive relationships: Involvement in relationships that are physically, sexually or emotionally oppressive and abusive. Being the caretaker of an addict in a relationship. Using sex as the only indicator of closeness in a relationship. Difficulty communicating. Feeling an overwhelming need to control the relationship. Sexual dysfunction or lack of healthy sexuality in the relationship. Feeling lonely in the relationship. Repeated attraction to dysfunctional partners. Secrets in a relationship and lack of honesty.

Abstinence from relationships or dating: Fearing sexual intimacy because of past experiences. Being celibate or virginal into adulthood. Fearful of sexual encounter. Abstaining from dating relationships or social romantic interaction.

Excessive sexual acting out (sexual addiction): One-night sexual affairs. Sexual acting out outside of marital or significant relationships. Emotional affairs outside of marital or significant relationships (an affair which lacks only the act of physical sex). Sexualizing members of the opposite sex (seeing women or men as only sexual playthings). Inappropriate or seductive dressing. Excessive sexual joking or innuendo. Involvement with pornographic magazines or movies. Frequenting strip joints, adult book stores, peeping-Tom behaviors or flashing. Excessive masturbation. Masturbation replacing sexual activity with a significant relationship. Sadomasochistic behavior. Involvement in bondage sex. Frequenting prostitutes or escort services. Sex with animals. Rape. Child molesting or incest.

Sex role confusion: Concern about being homosexual. Not having a clear cut sexual identity. Knowing about males or females but not knowing how to be male or female. Acting out bisexually and not feeling comfortable with sexual behavior. Having shame about behavior.

Addictive disorders: Addiction to alcohol, drugs, food, sex, work, people, religion, rage. Feeling incomplete and looking for someone or something to fill up emptiness. Using addictive behavior to avoid feelings, anger, grief, shame, loneliness. Denial about addictive behavior. Minimizing impact of addictive behavior on self or others. Having been confronted by a family member about addictive behavior but refusing to acknowledge it.

Physical and psychosomatic difficulties: Urinary tract infections starting at an early age. Gastrointestinal difficulties. Migraine headaches. A history of asthma. Insomnia. Excessive vaginal and bladder infections.

Unexplained depressions: Feeling down, low, sad, blue for unexplained reasons. Feeling as though life is not worth living. Wondering why life exists and what the purpose of living is. Talking about suicide, planning suicide, attempting suicide.

Excessive masturbation during childhood: Masturbating regularly. Masturbating to get to sleep. Masturbating when lonely, angry or bored.

Excessive sexual acting out during childhood: Excessive touching of other children's genitals. Mutual masturbation. Attempting sexual intercourse with same or opposite sexed children. Sexual acting out between siblings. Excessive use of sexual innuendo or joking.

Killing or hurting animals during childhood: Beating, kicking or hurting birds, cats, dogs, rabbits, etc. Fascination with injuring or killing animals. Setting fire to animals or insects.

Fear of same or opposite sex: Seeing all men or women as the same: all men being only after sex or all women being nags. Difficulty establishing healthy same sexed relationships. Homophobic, fear of homosexuality, homosexuals or lesbians. Difficulty establishing healthy opposite-sexed relationships. Only being able to have relationships with the opposite sex, being male or female dependent.

Overwhelming sense of shame: Feeling inadequate. Fearing others will find out secrets about self. Strong need to cover up inadequacies. Strong need for control and perfection. The impostor syndrome, feeling like a fake. Not knowing self. Taking on roles or behaviors to cover up lack of self-esteem.

Many have been sexually abused but have repressed any memory of childhood trauma, and many of us have memories of our abuse, but do not see the abuse as sexual because of a lack of awareness and education about what is sexually abusive. A number of us become very defensive when a therapist, friend or relative suggests we have been sexually abused because we immediately think sexual abuse only means intercourse with an adult during childhood. Though intercourse with an adult during childhood is certainly sexually abusive, it is only one example of sexual abuse. There are two categories of sexual abuse:

1. direct sexual abuse.
2. indirect sexual abuse.

Direct sexual abuse is abuse which is a consequence of a lack of awareness of healthy boundaries.

Indirect Sexual Abuse

A lack of privacy or boundaries: Adults not closing the door when they are using the bathroom. Adults not covering up with a robe or dressing appropriately. Mother walking around in bra, panties, skimpy nightgown or father in underwear. Exposure in excess to parents in the nude. Parents not closing or locking door when sexually engaged. Not allowing children privacy while dressing or using the bathroom. Showering or bathing with children after toddler age. Children sleeping with parents on a consistent basis. Exposure to adult pornography.

Living with parents who are sexually inappropriate: Living with parents who are involved in extramarital affairs. Living with a single parent who is sexually addicted and involved in excessive casual sex. Exposure to an adult's pornographic magazine or movie collection.

Shamed for being male or female: Being told a boy was wanted instead of you. Being told all women are either whores or madonnas. Shaming comments made about breast development or genital size. Being shamed for having sexual feelings. Having dating or opposite-sexed relationships overcontrolled.

Face slapping: Our face is part of our identity in that it shows others who we are as sexual beings. It is sexually shaming to be slapped in the face.

Enemas or other intrusive medical procedures: These are sexually intrusive and abusive, even when they are necessary because these procedures are humiliating and shaming.

Living with parents who have difficulty with their own sexuality: Living with parents who have sex-role confusion. Living with parents who appear to be repressed sexually, never touching, never kissing, sleeping in separate rooms. Living with parents who have unresolved sexual abuse issues.

Inappropriate sexual information: Little or lack of information about sexual development. Too much information about sexual development too soon.

Emotional incest: Being put in the position of surrogate spouse with a parent. Hearing about adult problems. Being exposed to adult sexual difficulties. Being set up to be Mama's little man or Daddy's little princess. Being expected to side with one parent during a parental disagreement. Being set up to protect one parent from another. Being told to relay messages from one parent to another.

Emotional incest can be incredibly damaging, causing confusion in establishing intimate opposite-sexed relationships in adulthood. Emotional incest forces children to abandon the role of child and assume or take the place of an adult. When this happens, it is not in the child's best interest. It is the need of the parent or adult who places a child in the role of surrogate spouse, playmate, protector or, in some cases, lover.

JODY'S STORY | Jody was a bright cheerful little girl who was full of energy. Everybody in the family thought Jody was special, but her father thought she was more than special. Jody and her father were together constantly and he referred to her as his little princess. He traveled a lot on business. Usually her mother did not want to go so Jody would accompany her father. She would go with him on his business calls during the day and have fancy dinners with him at night. He would always buy her something special on these trips and she would feel very grown up.

Jody's mother felt uneasy with her husband's indulging behavior with their daughter. At times she even felt jealous of the attention Jody received. She wished her husband would sometimes show *her* the attention he so willingly gave his daughter. She and Jody had always had conflict in their relationship. As a mother she felt power-less to discipline her daughter because her husband would intervene and sabotage her efforts to set guidelines and limits. She found herself disliking her daughter more and more and began pulling away emotionally. She felt as if Jody and her father shared a secret world in which she was not allowed to enter and she resented it.

Jody is a victim of emotional incest. She and her father have the type of intimacy in their relationship which is reserved for adults. Because her father has difficulty hav-ing a healthy intimate relationship with his wife, he has set Jody up to fulfill those needs for him. Jody has been abused with empowerment, and though this empower-ment makes her feel "more grown up," it has also robbed her of her childhood. Her mother and father have paved the path for her to care for the needs of others in return for approval and affection, and she will continue this pattern in adulthood. Children should receive approval and affection without having to pay such a price.

Jody is being cheated out of a mother because she is in direct competition with her for her father's attention. Jody's mother is jealous of the relationship between Jody and her father which makes it difficult for her to be a caring nurturing mother. Both parents are at fault for putting Jody in the middle of their relationship. Jody is a buffer between two adults who need to be addressing their own unresolved issues. Jody will have difficulty establishing healthy male or female relationships in adulthood as a consequence. She has been set up to compete with women and not trust them. Jody is also at risk for being dependent on men to make her feel worthwhile.

Emotional incest is finally being recognized by helping professionals as a damaging and abusive consequence of unhealthy boundaries within a dysfunctional family. In adulthood individuals who have suffered from emotional incest have to "divorce" the parent who empowered them for their own recovery. As long as they continue to serve the role of surrogate mate for this parent, they are not free to experience healthy intimate relationships. The empowering parent continues to depend on the emotionally incested individual for those needs which he or she is not able to have taken care of in healthy ways.

The divorce begins by slowly saying no to the empowering parent and by setting limits. Statements such as "Oh, you don't love me" or "You don't care anymore" are common and the process is extremely difficult. There is a fear of being rejected by the empowering parent and at times a fear of being rejected by the other parent as well.

Sometimes the other parent also needs to have the emotional incest continue. In Jody's case her mother was invested in the emotional incest continuing because she disliked traveling with her husband on business trips. She was allowing the abuse to continue by neither assuming her role as spouse nor addressing the issue of traveling with her husband. Instead, she encouraged her daughter to take her place, during which time she did not have to confront her husband.

The World Of Adults

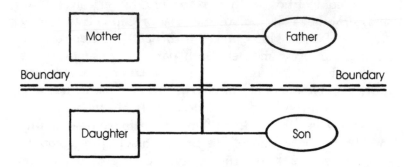

Boundary ———————————————— Boundary

The World Of Children

Children need to be children and not cross over into the world of adulthood until age-appropriate.

Figure 3.1. Healthy Family

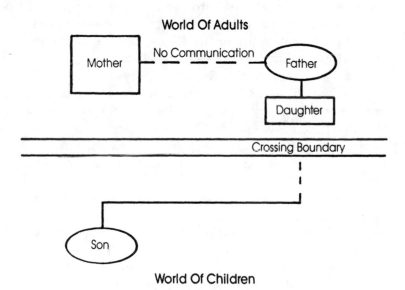

World Of Adults

Crossing Boundary

World Of Children

Figure 3.2. Unhealthy Family
(Emotional Incest)

Many have stated, "My empowering parent has passed on. How can the emotional incest still be affecting me?" Even if a parent has died, it is still important to address the remaining scars of emotional incest. If not, the effects of such abuse will continue to disrupt healthy intimate relationships.

In some situations emotional incest moves towards physical incest and the role of surrogate spouse includes sexual partner.

Many of us have a number of misconceptions about what exactly constitutes sexual abuse. Also a number of helping professionals have a lack of awareness about behaviors considered sexually abusive. In some emotionally incestuous relationships between a child and parent, direct sexual abuse with intent and purpose can take place. Direct sexual abuse, as opposed to indirect sexual abuse, is intentional and its purpose is to fulfill the sexual needs of the adult. In most situations, direct sexual abuse occurs with someone the child knows. When this happens, children are confused, wondering why this person is "touching me there" or "rubbing me like that." Children are naturally self-centered, believing their parents and the world rotates around them. They also have a lot of creative magical thinking which helps them understand the world in which they live.

Setting Limits

My son, Aaron, loves baseball and as a toddler he was totally engrossed in the sport. He talked baseball constantly and would only wear shoes with cleats "like the big baseball players." Luckily for my hardwood floor, I found plastic cleats for him. Aaron in his love for baseball truly believed that I was just as excited about baseball as he was. I had grown up with a father who played professional baseball and as a consequence of this, had a great deal of unresolved grief about the price I had paid for my father's baseball career.

Being the adult child of alcoholics I was, I naturally wanted to be the perfect parent. I worked on my own unfinished business with my father's career and made peace with the sport of baseball. My husband, Aaron and I went to baseball games, played baseball, bought baseballs, bats, clothes and cards, and knew the names of most major league stars. I began to feel my world rotating around my son and baseball and realized his desires as a toddler were insatiable. I discovered he naturally believed the world rotated around him. To my horror, I discovered my husband and I had been overempowering Aaron by not setting limits with our emotional and financial resources with respect to baseball. (Aaron could not understand why I did not want a pair of cleats.)

As Michael and I began setting limits on some of the baseball activity within the Brandon household, I would ask Aaron periodically if he knew why we were not playing baseball as often as we used to. One of his responses was "Because Daddy won't let you play, Mama." I asked him why Daddy wouldn't let me play and he responded with "Because you're in trouble." Aaron did not have the maturity to understand the concept of limit-setting, and so with magical thinking, he used past experience to make sense out of this situation. In the past if Aaron was having a tantrum, we would take time out from baseball as a disciplinary measure. So Aaron naturally thought I was not playing baseball as much as I had in the past because I was in trouble or in time-out.

When children do not understand the experiences they have and when these experiences are not clarified for them by an adult, they will use magical thinking to make sense of them. Their magical thinking will incorporate denial, rationalization, minimization and other defenses to make the world around them a safe and logical place to live in.

Naturally self-centered children, when sexually abused, will logically believe they have done something to bring on the abuse. They will feel responsible and utilize magical thinking to make sense of the experience. Children may believe they have been abused because they did something wrong and are being punished. In other instances the belief may be that it is their job to take care of the abuser because the abuser is sad, mad or lonely.

Children are in many cases told not to tell "because it would upset Mommy or Daddy." In most situations children believe the abusers know what they are doing because physically they are much bigger. In a number of cases the sexual abuse is stimulating and pleasurable, and with magical thinking, children decide the experience was appropriate because "it felt good."

When a child is sexually abused, the nonverbal messages they receive are:

- "You have no rights."
- "Your body is not your own."
- "I am right, you are wrong."
- "I am doing this for your own good."
- "You have done something to deserve this."
- "You do not have a right to protection."
- "You really want this experience."
- "You're special and this is why we are doing this."
- "This is normal."
- "It's your fault; I can't help myself."

A child's chances for developing healthy boundaries are completely destroyed when he or she is sexually abused. The above messages are carried on into adulthood and the ability to care for self in healthy positive ways is lost. If there is memory loss of the abusive experience, the messages received as a consequence of the abuse continue, creating difficulty and hardship in adult life.

Direct sexual abuse takes on many forms and in some cases, disguises. The following are examples of direct sexual abuse:

- Exposure to pornographic movies or magazines by an older person.
- Inappropriate touching, hugging, kissing or dancing with an older person which feels wrong, bad, scary or icky.
- Exposure by an older person to adult sexual activities, such as acts of sex, sexual games, bars, strip joints, adult book stores, prostitution.
- Being masturbated or being used for masturbation.

- Being penetrated vaginally or anally with fingers or other implements.
- Being forced or seduced into performing oral sex.
- Being forced or seduced into performing anal sex or intercourse.
- Rape as an adult or during childhood is sexually abusive.
- Using acts of sex as a way of nurturing a child.
- Setting children up to believe since the act of sex was pleasurable, the offenders involved were not in the wrong.
- Being told not to tell.
- Being fondled or touched inappropriately under the guise of bathing, lap sitting, having clothes tucked in, while being put to bed.
- Being fondled or touched sexually while being tickled or rough-housing.
- Being encouraged or forced to act out sexually with other children.
- Being forced to participate in satanic rituals.

The children involved in ritualistic abuse have been horribly traumatized. Recently more victims of such abuse are beginning to share how they were in many cases sexually, physically, spiritually and emotionally abused. A number of them have witnessed animal and even human sacrifices. Many victims fear sharing history such as this for fear of being rejected or discounted. Others have buried these memories deep within in order to survive the terror they endured. With specific help, recovery and healing is possible. There is a national organization for those affected by satanic ritual abuse, and if you suspect you are a victim of such abuse, I strongly recommend you contact:

Cult Awareness Network
2421 W. Pratt Blvd., Suite 1173
Chicago, IL 60645
(312) 267-7777

When a child is emotionally, physically, spiritually or sexually abused without help for such trauma, chances for developing healthy boundaries are very limited. Children learn about boundaries and self-care by watching how adults treat them, other adults and themselves. Our beliefs and values about the world are initially developed by interacting with the adults within our childhood environment. If children are raised with healthy guidelines, positive physical touch and nurturing, they will be able to develop those tools necessary for a successful adult life. These adults will be able to move freely along the path of life with all of its bumps, lumps, joys and challenges while at the same time learning, growing and evolving. For those of us who have been abused, the path of life can be confusing, frustrating and lonely, giving us a sense that life is always to be a struggle.

For those of us from dysfunctional families, it is difficult to know what our lessons are and at times impossible to see their value because we have not been given the tools necessary for successfully resolving pain and conflict. Most of us feel stuck and find ourselves repeating old familiar patterns over and over again. The sad news is this is a consequence of unresolved trauma. Attention to our unfinished business is needed for resolution. The glad news is there is a way out.

The Fear Of Abandonment

| 4

I live along the Gulf Coast of Texas where hurricanes are commonplace. During my years of residence in this area I had never suffered any major loss as a consequence of storm damage until Hurricane Chantal hit the shores of Texas.

Being somewhat of a crisis junkie, when hearing about the approach of an oncoming hurricane I would busy myself by cooking large quantities of food, preparing for the worst, all the while projecting into the future about loss of property or life as a consequence of tornadoes, floods or even a tidal wave. Usually the damage incurred for me and my family after one of these big wind and rain blasts was minimal . . . until Chantal.

When Chantal hit our area, I was on my usual crisis junkie high, making beef stew while watching broken tree branches and other debris blow down the street. My husband, Michael, who is also a crisis junkie, was busy pacing the house with a flashlight looking for leaks.

During hurricanes or other times of major stress, both of us will revert back to childhood behavior. I become a clinging vine, very needy of attention and reassurance. Michael builds thick barriers around himself, not wanting to talk or be comforted in any way. As far as boundaries go, neither of us has any that are healthy at times like this.

We usually end up nagging at one another. He will accuse me of acting childlike and I will call him a cold fish. What is really happening during these times of intense stress is that both of us are fearing abandonment. I become as I was during childhood, fearing I will be left all alone with no protection or support. My fear of abandonment during Chantal was at an all-time high, especially as I watched Michael withdraw into his world of inner isolation.

Michael, watching me revert from a confident woman into a helpless child, began to feel my lack of support, demanding that he protect me. He felt emotionally abandoned and pulled away for protection. The more barriers he built, the more demanding for attention I became. We both pushed one another further and further into dysfunction as a consequence of our own fears of abandonment.

For Michael it was safer to withdraw and isolate than to feel being emotionally abandoned by me. This is what he had done in childhood. Under intense stress, many of us tend to revert back to our old childhood survival skills. I had rarely been protected emotionally, physically or sexually as a child, and during times of stress would still look to someone, usually Michael, to fix it and make it better. Since I had rarely been protected as a child, I would still look for protectors in adult life during times of stress.

After Chantal passed, we went outside, raked up tree branches and hugged each other in relief, while making amends to one another for our dysfunctional behavior during the storm. I talked about how I felt abandoned by him as he isolated and Michael shared how he felt the same, watching me emotionally regress.

We thought all was well until our building manager called to tell us our office had been hit by a tornado and not to come to the office building. Of course we jumped right into our car and raced straight over to our office. What a sight! The roof was on the floor and water was everywhere. Both Michael and I wept as we stood in four inches of water, looking at the holes in our ceiling. Both of us felt the loss of our home away from home, and the feeling of total powerlessness was overwhelming. I felt like I was four years old, all alone in the world, unprotected from the traumas of life. At that moment I felt abandoned by my Higher Power and very vulnerable. In actuality, emotionally I was four years old and was re-experiencing what it felt like to be an abused, abandoned four-year-old.

As a four-year-old I had been abandoned by the higher powers (adults) in my environment and had not been protected. The trauma of Chantal pulled up for me out of my inner self many of my own unresolved abandonment fears. As a consequence, my childlike whining and clinging began.

Michael, on the flip side of this situation, was withdrawing more and more. I could tell he was in pain, even felt his pain, and he was having difficulty sharing any of it. He began busily organizing the wet ceiling tiles on the floor while I sat on a wet chair and moaned. Neither of us was able to offer support to the other. Our once healthy boundaries were nonexistent, and our abandonment feelings had kicked in for the second time that day.

As I watched my creature comforts float around the office, I wished someone or something would fix this mess and realized this is how I often felt in my family of origin. I remembered being angry with God, wondering why I had been put in such a sick family. In early recovery I had raged at God about my childhood predicament, only to learn that my anger was really about feeling abandoned by my parents. Eventually I learned it wasn't God's fault that I had been abused and abandoned. I discovered my abuse and abandonment was the consequence of generations of addiction.

Several days after the shock of the tornado damage, I raged at Hurricane Chantal for destroying my office and upsetting my life. I took responsibility for my feelings and experienced my grief on the loss of my home away from home. By parenting myself with love and kindness I was able to have my feelings about my loss and heal from the trauma.

I also took several days off from being a helping professional to allow Carla to take care of Carla.

I was able to nurture my own child within who still
had feelings about being abandoned. By setting boundaries for myself, I was giving to myself the gift of healing
and protection.

Michael's walls eventually came down, and he allowed
himself to sit in his sadness for several days. He would
share with me and others how Hurricane Chantal had
affected him. Michael set a boundary periodically with me
during this time and asked for space to be in his feelings.
At other times he would accept comforting and help. We
both mourned the loss of our building by having our anger
and grief individually and together. At the same time we
were able to examine our unfinished business around our
abandonment fears. Life periodically offers us opportunities for growth but those opportunities can feel like the
end of the world. They can also provide us with a second
chance at healing.

Secrets

I believe the feeling of abandonment is a core issue for
most individuals who come from dysfunctional families. I
also feel that the severity of this core issue determines
our ability to develop healthy boundaries in adult life.
Little children fear being left all alone in the world and
depend on those adults around them to be there emotionally and physically for protection. When a child wonders if
a parent will leave them, the first question that comes to
mind is, "Who will take care of me? Who will protect me?
Who will love me?"

When children are abandoned emotionally or physically
as a result of addiction, emotional, physical, sexual or spiritual abuse, death, parental divorce, loss of a sibling, long-
term parental illness, war or any other family trauma, the
consequences are abandonment issues in adulthood.

Children will respond to abandonment in several ways.
If the family trauma is not discussed, it becomes a secret.
My parents divorced when I was 11, and I remember

being told, "Don't tell the neighbors. We don't want to air our laundry in public." I thought to myself, "Divorce must be a sin or something, otherwise I could talk about it." Since I didn't want the neighbors to think my family was sinful or bad, I never told anyone about my parents' divorce for quite a while.

Little kids use magical thinking to make sense out of the world when it isn't properly explained to them. I remember feeling a great deal of pain about my father not living with us, even wondering if I had done something wrong to make him move out.

I was in a school play on Father's Day, and we sang a song for the parents in the audience called *Oh, My Papa*. I can remember crying while singing this song. With only my mother in the audience, I felt all alone in the world without my father in attendance. The reason for my parents' divorce remained a mystery for some time, and I remember my sisters and I trying to comfort both of our parents, hoping if we were good enough both parents would be there for us.

Vulnerability

Periodically, parents will come to our office with complaints about their children. The complaints usually center on dropping grades, chemical usage, acting-out behavior, stealing or other dysfunctional behavior. Most of these parents comment at one time or another, "Suzy was such a good girl" or "Billy never used to do this before." When children are abandoned or fear being abandoned, they believe it is in response to their behavior. If the situation is not explained to them several times, in age-appropriate language, they will use magical thinking to develop a system of coping skills for surviving the trauma.

One system of survival involves always being good. With these children, adults usually do not notice there is a difficulty and comments are made about "How well Sarah is taking her parents' divorce. She's a model student" or "How grown up Johnny is being about the death of his father" or "Look at what a help George is to his mother with his alcoholic father" or "Look at how well Jody has come through the abuse that occurred in her family. She has her head on straight." In reality, all of the above are dysfunctional responses to abandonment within the family of origin. These children have each made the trauma a consequence of something they have done, and in response to fearing abandonment, are "being good" for fear of being left all alone in the world with nobody to care for them.

Perfectionism

Sarah believes if her grades are good enough, her mother will love her more and maybe allow her father to come home. Sarah also believes if her grades are good enough, her father will be so proud of her that he will *want* to come home. Sarah will grow up into an adult who will rarely feel she is good enough. She will not know how to enjoy her success and will usually be attaining her goals for others. She will have difficulty saying no to others and will find herself in relationships where she is constantly giving. She will fear saying no and not giving at all times because she fears abandonment in her adult relationships. She will succeed in getting the approval of others, fearing nobody will like her if she is not perfect. Sarah will not know how to set boundaries with people who want to take advantage of her, and periodically she will feel victimized.

Over-Responsibility

JOHNNY'S STORY | Johnny fears having feelings about the loss of his father because he has been told his mother needs him to be strong. Johnny has also been told he is now the man of the house and that it is his job to take his father's place. Johnny is angry with God and wonders why God took his father from him. When he mentions how he feels about God, he is told, "God knows best and it isn't your place to judge." Johnny believes God has abandoned him and also feels abandoned by his father.

He feels scared because he doesn't feel he can fill his father's shoes. Johnny knows his mother cannot comfort him because she is too upset, and he doesn't want to cause her any more pain by complaining. In the back of his mind, he now fears his mother may die, too, and wonders who would be there for him then. Johnny works very hard to do the right thing and be strong for his mother. He knows that she can't be there for him when he has problems, but at least she is still there physically.

In adult life, Johnny has difficulty with close relationships. He never wants to become too intimate because he fears he will just be abandoned eventually anyway. He believes one can't really trust people. He has difficulty risking closeness with others and rarely shares his true self with anyone. He keeps to himself, never sharing too much.

He doesn't believe in God and feels he has only himself to depend on. Johnny believes that it is easier for him to just "do it himself" when confronted with problems and has little faith in the ability of others. As he doesn't believe in asking for help, he can't understand why some people need to talk about their problems.

He has difficulty around people who are emotional and sees them as over-reactive and immature. Pain is viewed as a weakness, and he would never consider crying in front of someone!

Johnny will have difficulty experiencing an intimate relationship with anyone. He will also not be able to heal from life's traumas. Periodically he will feel lonely and incomplete, but will cover these feelings up with some addictive behavior, such as work, sex or alcohol.

Chances are he will find himself in relationships with partners who need caretaking. He will feel it is his job to make them happy and will do as asked at all times for fear of not being liked or even abandoned. Johnny will enable his alcoholic friends, take care of needy women, along with dysfunctional business partners, and rarely express his feelings about their behavior for fear of upsetting them. Having difficulty setting boundaries with others, he will avoid his pain about being used or abused in his relationships by building walls of numbness around himself. His ability to trust will be limited, and he will have a difficult time accepting or asking for help. Johnny's need for control will overwhelm those around him at times and cause difficulty in his significant relationships.

My mother died when I was 16, and I had tremendous abandonment fears. I fluctuated from not having any boundaries at all, allowing myself to be used to isolating from the world, not wanting to risk possible abandonment.

I remember when my son was born, I was fearful of loving him too much and becoming really attached. I was scared I would grow to love him completely and then he would die. For the first year of his life I never allowed myself to enjoy him totally, fearing my feelings of abandonment should he become sick and die. This interfered with my ability to be a healthy mother.

In other significant relationships I would allow myself to be abused, victimized and used. I feared standing up for myself because I believed I would be left all alone if I did. I had to re-experience the feelings of being left by my father as a consequence of divorce and by my mother as a result of her early death in order to develop healthy boundaries in adulthood. Today I can be close to my child and risk loving him totally. I don't have to withhold my feelings for fear of becoming too close. I can also stand up for myself and say, "No! Don't hurt me. I will protect myself and not allow it."

Resolving old abandonment issues teaches us how to be a part of the world, experiencing it to the fullest, while at the same time being safe and secure.

Absence Of Same-Sexed Parent

George is growing up with an alcoholic father. As a consequence of his father's alcoholism, he isn't receiving the fathering he needs which would allow him to develop healthy intimate relationships with males. He will also have difficulty being a father himself because his own father was a dysfunctional role model.

He will be confused about his own maleness because his father, due to his alcoholism, was unavailable to teach him how to care for himself as a male. George may have difficulty taking care of his basic needs, finding it difficult to take himself to the doctor when sick or to the dentist for annual checkups. He may feel at a loss when he is in need of new socks, shirts or other articles of clothing, not really knowing how to shop for himself. Our same-sexed parent models for us how to care for and love ourselves. If our same-sexed parent is addicted, absent or dysfunctional in any way, we will have difficulty knowing how to care for ourselves as adults. We may know how to do for others, but we will have confusion about doing for ourselves.

Abuse Survivor

Jody comes from a family where there was sexual and physical abuse. Her mother sexually and physically abused her on a regular basis. She tried to tell other relatives about the abuse but their response to her was that she was just imagining things. Jody was told to stop telling such awful lies and to pull herself together. She was also told by relatives that since her father had died, her mother was having a difficult time and to be strong for her mother. Jody's mother would sleep with her and touch her inappropriately during the night. Jody tried to ignore the touching.

Her mother would also discipline her with the belt when angry, telling her if she cried, she would receive more whippings. Jody learned to numb her body physically while being sexually or physically abused and would escape her mother's chaotic behavior with her schoolwork. She made excellent grades, and her teachers marveled at how well she appeared to have adjusted to the loss of her father. Jody's friends thought her mother was nuts but admired how strong Jody was.

In adult life Jody becomes involved with men who hit her. When she is hit, she numbs her body and avoids the physical pain. She avoids her emotional pain by working 70 hours a week and by having a couple of drinks after work to unwind. She is at the top of her business firm and is respected by all of her peers.

Jody lives a double life. She appears confident and together to the public but her personal life is full of abuse
and addiction. Since she numbs out the abuse inflicted
upon her in her personal life, she will have difficulty seeing the seriousness of her situation. She fears letting
anyone know how vulnerable she really is and feels like an
imposter when peers at work share their admiration with
her for her skills.

Shutting Down

Abuse survivors survive abuse by shutting down and
numbing out both physically and emotionally. In adulthood
many have difficulty feeling their feelings and continue to
block out the physical or emotional pain inflicted upon
them by others. Pain forces us to take action, and if we do
not experience our pain, we will remain in the problem,
not seeking solutions. Those of us who block our pain are
unaware that we are in need of help for our painful situations or relationships.

At times abuse survivors will come to my office with
concerns about difficulty in adult life. At some point they
will share with me about their intimate relationships.
They will describe emotionally, physically or sexually abusive situations which sound terrifying, and when I react
with concern, they will be surprised. My reaction to their
situation will seem over-reactive to them because they
are so out of touch with the seriousness of their abuse.
This is a very common response for abuse survivors who
know how to block pain.

It is impossible to know how to set boundaries with
others and care for self when we are out of touch with
our own pain. By blocking our emotional and physical
pain, we are abandoning ourselves just as we were abandoned by those adults around us in childhood. We are
allowing the cycle of abuse to continue when we do not
set boundaries with those in our adult life who are emotionally, physically or sexually hurting and abusing us. It is
our responsibility to learn how to feel all of our feelings
by being in touch with ourselves both emotionally and

physically. If this sounds difficult or impossible, do not lose hope as we will be addressing ways in which to do this in the workbook section of this book.

Those of us who have been abandoned as a consequence of family of origin dysfunction react in several ways. Many of us attempt to be as *good* as possible, hoping people will love us enough to be available to us in times of need, not leaving us alone in the world. As a result in adulthood we allow ourselves to be disempowered, used and abused by others, always doing and giving to all, never knowing we have a right to care for and protect ourselves.

Others of us learn in early childhood that our world is totally unsafe and that it is our responsibility to protect and care for ourselves because nobody else in our environment will do it for us. We develop an attitude which says to others, "Don't trust anybody" or "Never ask for help, do it yourself" or "Never show your vulnerability" or "Men are only after one thing" or "Women will just use you" or "Don't let anyone know who you really are because they will just use it against you." At this end of the spectrum, the belief is that people will only hurt us. This belief usually originates in early childhood in response to trauma and loss. When there isn't any protection from the pain of youth, children will learn how to protect themselves with the help of magical thinking.

Fantasy Barrier

SCOTT'S STORY | In Scott's house his parents were always yelling at one another. Scott hated these times and could never understand why his parents didn't resolve their problems. His mother was always complaining about something, usually his father's work schedule. One time Scott even heard his mother accusing his father of having a girlfriend. His parents would rage at one another late into the night. During these times Scott would go into his closet with his flashlight and read. Here he could escape into the safe fantasy world of Robin Hood and His Merry Men or live through the eyes of Batman conquering the evil and criminal minds in Gotham City. Sometimes he fell asleep in the closet and neither of his parents seemed to mind him not being in his bed at night.

Scott doesn't have many friends and considers himself a loner. With a crowd he can tell jokes and goof off like the other kids, but he never shares what he really feels or what his home life is really like, rarely inviting friends to his home.

When Scott reaches adulthood, he will most likely use fantasy to avoid his life problems. Fantasy for Scott is an emotional barrier which protects him from the pain in his childhood environment.

Many children will isolate themselves with fantasy when confronted with their parents' dysfunction. It isn't safe at these times of intense family stress to be completely aware of how dysfunctional parents really are. With the aid of magical thinking, fantasy provides the necessary escape from reality.

Children such as this usually survive by developing one of several emotional barriers. They either work towards becoming invisible, blocking out all pain experienced in their environment or they rebel by acting out all of the dysfunction within the family system, then distance themselves from others with inappropriate behavior.

Scott wants to be invisible during times of pain and conflict. When his parents are raging at each other, neither is available to care for Scott's emotional well-being. Raging behavior is abusive to children because it is frightening and intimidating. When parents are raging, their best interests are not for the children involved, and the children feel abandoned, alone and scared. It is acceptable and even encouraged that adults disagree in front of children to model appropriate conflict resolution skills, but raging behavior is not an appropriate method of conflict resolution.

Scott is intimidated by his parents' behavior and finds safety within his world of fantasy. He will be intimidated with angry people in adulthood and will have difficulty with conflict. He will abandon himself, his opinions and needs in order to avoid conflict.

Individuals, such as Scott, usually look in control on the outside, and comments from peers about them may be, "He's always so in control" or "Nothing ever seems to rattle him" or "I don't know how she feels, she'll never really say" or "We can always depend on her for stability."

Living Behind Barriers

The need to appear in control is overwhelming, and the word *vulnerable* has very negative connotations because to be in control insures a false sense of safety.

I asked one individual who was having marital difficulties if she had shared her concerns about her relationship with her spouse, and her reply was, "I wouldn't dream of telling him how I feel. He might use it against me. I don't want him to know how vulnerable I am."

Another shared with me, "I can't tell her how I am feeling. You want me to expose myself? I have difficulty even admitting my feelings to myself, let alone her."

Barriers are built to insulate us not only from others, but even from ourselves. This barrier can be a wall of fantasy or even addiction, and it provides a temporary feeling of false security and safety. For many it provides a form of surrogate parenting.

For myself, my addictions kept me insulated from the real world. With alcohol the reality of my past pain was blunted. Michael, my husband, masked for himself the pain of my alcoholism with workaholism, rarely ever having to experience the pain which was so apparent in our relationship.

For many years we were both invisible to the other in our relationship until our addictions had progressed to a point where the dysfunction could no longer be ignored. During those years of addiction we avoided our individual pain about being abandoned by one another. In our delusion we were unaware of how our addictive barriers kept us from experiencing any true communication and intimacy. People who live behind barriers for safety as a consequence of childhood trauma can never build healthy intimacy with self or others until the walls which kept them safe for so long begin to tumble down. Our vulnerability must be expressed in order for us to heal and connect in healthy ways with ourselves and others. We will still need some protection for our emotional well-being, but our new mode of protection must be more flexible than the isolating barriers developed with magical thinking in childhood.

The Scapegoat

Many children build up layers of protection from feelings of fear, loneliness and abandonment by distancing themselves with rebellious, inappropriate and even hostile behavior.

For years specialists in recovery have labeled this role the scapegoat. Some children in dysfunctional family systems act out negatively for attention, even if that attention is not at all positive. The thought is that negative attention for children such as these was better than no attention at all. Though I agree with this concept, I believe the goals involved are a few more than meet the eye.

PATTY'S STORY | Patty's parents were divorced when she was seven years old, and she went to live with her father. Patty's mother disappeared and Patty never saw her again in childhood. Patty was confused, hurt, lonely and angry and could not understand why her mother had left her. Living with her father was very scary because her father was an alcoholic. When Patty's father drank too much, his behavior was unpredictable. Sometimes he would call her by her mother's name, crying, while at other times he would rage at her and curse. When her father was sober, he would not interact with her at all and would even distance himself from her. Patty learned how to protect herself from his extreme mood swings by ignoring him and knew it was never safe to trust him.

At times Patty felt all alone in the world but had decided she didn't need anybody and that all she had to depend on was herself. She made a decision that she would never let anyone ever hurt her the way her mother and father had hurt her. She also vowed that she would make something out of herself and be a success in adult life.

Patty will grow up with barriers full of distrust and caution. She will question the motives of all and rarely self-disclose her innermost feelings, opinions or attitudes, especially if they were to expose her vulnerability. Her relationships will be superficial, and addiction will provide her with temporary escape from her loneliness. She may use food to nurture herself, chemicals to insulate herself from pain, work to provide a false sense of self-esteem or sex to cover up her loneliness.

Patty has been abandoned by first her mother and then by her father. Her mother physically and emotionally abandoned her, and Patty, not understanding her mother's behavior, decided to just ignore it. By ignoring her mother's behavior she did not have to experience her feelings of abandonment. When her friends would ask her about her mother, she would reply angrily that she hated her mother and was glad she was gone. She would refer to her mother as a witch who hit her and was mean to her, even though her mother never hit her.

When children are abandoned emotionally or physically, they may react with rebellion towards the person who has left them, even if the abandonment is a consequence of death. In many cases it is easier to feel feelings of anger and hostility about being abandoned, than the sad lonely feelings of grief from the significant loss.

If children do not have healthy support and guidance for experiencing this rage, it may be acted out in self-destructive activities, which distance one from the intense feelings of loss. Then healing is impossible. Walls of distrust and rage push away intimate relationships, insulating the child within from the possibility of future abandonment. Children may act out feelings of abandonment with fighting, anti-social behavior, school truancy, sexual acting out, chemical usage, negativism and oppositional behavior.

Patty's father also has abandoned her. By not resolving his relationship with his ex-wife and with his continued alcoholism, he is emotionally unavailable to care for his daughter. By referring to her by his ex-wife's name and raging at her for her mother's behavior, he has inappropriately misdirected his anger. Patty has justified confusion about this because she is being blamed for her mother's activities. She feels angry with her mother for leaving her in this situation and angry with her father for blaming her.

At age 16 Patty runs away from home. She learns how to get what she needs by sleeping with men and soon becomes wise to the art of manipulation. Though she is involved in a number of relationships, none of them are emotionally satisfying. Patty can never trust anybody fully because she constantly fears their motives.

With scenarios such as the above, people like Patty can become successful business people, political leaders, strong religious leaders, humanitarians, prostitutes, drug dealers, criminals and more. There is a public personality which enables them to be successful in whatever their venture may be and at the same time protect them. There is also a private personality which is rarely exposed. At times the private personality is buried so deeply that even its owners are unaware of its presence.

One woman shared with me that she had to appear strong and in control because she felt shame and embarrassment when comforted or offered help. She stated she never trusted the motives of those who offered help. She would appear distant and aloof when compassion was offered, pushing their help away.

Fear Of Intimacy

It is not uncommon for those of us who fear trust to push away potentially intimate relationships with distant or even offensive behavior. Usually we are not aware of our distancing behavior with others, and at times may question why others feel rejected or hurt by our responses. If a relationship begins to feel too close, we may begin doing things that anger the other person, starting fights, not returning phone calls, breaking dates, playing the blame game and emotionally pulling away from the relationship. We may even push people into abandoning us with distancing and then say to ourselves, "See, she left. She really didn't care."

The underlying fear is, "If I get too close, I may get hurt." As long as relationships are not too involved, we feel safe. As soon as they become intimate, we feel scared. Our need for distance springs up from out of nowhere, and we leave our friends, spouses, lovers, children, co-workers or relatives wondering why we have pulled away.

Intimacy frightens most of us who came from dysfunctional families because it forces us to be vulnerable with one another. In early childhood being vulnerable usually resulted in feeling abandoned and alone. And in response to the fear of these feelings, protection was needed. With the wonderful magical mind of a child many of us have survived the dysfunction in our families of origin. A number of us are too vulnerable too often with unsafe people in unsafe situations. We are too trusting, not exercising enough caution when danger is near.

As children we survived by numbing our emotional and physical pain when exposed to abuse and chaos. Some of us went off into worlds of fantasy to avoid and escape the realities of our childhoods. Others of us even moved out of our bodies in order to completely detach ourselves from our painful environments. We minimize the pain we lived with and suppressed the memories of our sad childhoods, only to recreate many of our family of origin experiences in our current relationships in adulthood. We feel unprotected and victimized and wonder why we are used and abused so often by our mates, friends, co-workers and relatives. We believe our destiny is to give constantly of ourselves and fear the phrase "Don't be selfish."

Hiding Behind The False Self

Then there are those of us who fear the world and hide behind a false sense of security, hoping nobody will ever discover how really afraid and unsure we are. Our false self appears tough, confident and in control on the outside while our loneliness, buried deep within, battles with our false concept of reality. We try to fool ourselves into believing all is well behind those barriers which distance us from ourselves and others, but we cheat ourselves out of the joy of the full human experience. Fearing abandonment, we decide that to trust means certain doom, so we are overly cautious, never allowing ourselves to be totally open and vulnerable with another.

Most of us fluctuate from being totally vulnerable and exposed to closing off all intimate contact with others. We swing from trusting all to believing in none. We fear abandonment and crave intimacy and end up being abandoned and push away intimacy. We always feel out of balance, swinging from one extreme to another, wondering when this seesaw called life will level out.

It is possible to live in the world, being a part of life, while at the same time feeling protected and responsible for self. I thought I was always going to be either the world's victim with a lifelong membership to martyr's anonymous, or that I would have to become a hermit on an island, isolating from all relationships. I really didn't believe I had a choice in the matter and felt I was doomed to a life void of healthy relationships.

I remember reaching a point in my growth where I craved intimate relationships while at the same time dreaded them. I feared being used, abused and abandoned again and felt stuck, not knowing how to move from dysfunction to health. Today I have boundaries which allow me to be a part of the world, while at the same time protected. I can spot dangerous situations and take the responsible action necessary to protect myself.

When I began taking responsibility for myself, not all in my environment were happy for me. Those I had allowed to use and abuse me were confused and even angered by my new behavior. But as I set limits with others by saying no and caring for myself, I discovered I was no longer abandoning myself. I discarded the dysfunctional barriers I had used for protection and began experimenting with ideas of self-protection which were more flexible. I can have friendships with all kinds of people in various situations and know it is my responsibility not to allow myself to be victimized. As long as I do not abandon myself, I can be safe in the world.

The first step in beginning to develop healthy boundaries is to learn how not to abandon ourselves. As we learn to care for and love ourselves, we will quickly discover half of the battle for healthy recovery has been won. Intimacy, honesty and love with self breeds the possibility of future healthy relationships. As we begin to heal ourselves from within by becoming our own best friend, we slowly learn about friendships with others. As my own best friend, I can no longer allow myself to be used, abused or hurt by myself or by others. This realization brings the gift of freedom.

The Disempowered Victim | 5

As a consequence of family of origin abuse, children develop specific survival skills which allow them to survive the trauma, confusion and chaos which occurs within their families of origin. One mode of survival involves unconsciously or consciously blocking out physical and/or emotional pain. With this blocking behavior the seriousness of the dysfunction and abuse within the family system is avoided, while a sense of false security provides temporary safety for the mind. These survival skills, which work to protect us in childhood, are carried on into adulthood and continue to express themselves in our adult relationships, current family situations, and even in the workplace. Though these survival skills serve us well in childhood, they cause us tremendous grief in adulthood.

Disempowerment

One consequence of family of origin abuse and dysfunction is disempowerment (or *the feeling of total powerless-*

ness in choicemaking). Most of us who have been disempowered with childhood abuse are not even aware of the
number of choices we have in everyday situations. We
have survived abuse by numbing ourselves out in order
not to feel our childhood pain and never really learn about
the process of choicemaking.

When an abuse survivor is experiencing trauma, they
are totally absorbed in surviving that trauma and do not
have the option of exploring the different avenues life
offers. Survival may mean blocking the pain of harsh
words or avoiding the physical trauma of a blow to the
face or other body parts or numbing the shame of being
sexually touched, or even penetrated, by a caregiver.

Since children believe those adults in their environment
are always right, there is a feeling of powerlessness when
being abused because children will believe the reality of
those abusing them while doubting their own.

In other words, they will believe on one level that the
abuser knows what is best for them and that they somehow deserve the abusive experience. Even if their reality
tells them that something is wrong, while they are being
abused, they will have difficulty trusting their perceptions
because of the abuser's position of authority, which is a
natural consequence of their status as adults.

Many abuse survivors continue to believe they were somehow at fault for the abuse, deserving of the abuse and carry
this feeling of responsibility into adulthood. This feeling of
responsibility continues to be expressed within our adult
relationships. Many of us, when wronged, have difficulty
understanding we have been offended. We are constantly
asking questions, such as, "What did I do to cause her to
say that to me?" or "For him to drink like that?"

SUSAN'S | Susan was raised in a very chaotic family with an
STORY | alcoholic mother and father. Her father would go
to the bars several nights a week and come home after
they had closed at 2:00 a.m. Her mother would sit and
watch television while nursing several glasses of orange
juice and vodka until late into the night. Her parents rarely

communicated except when fighting and slept in separate rooms. At times Susan wondered why they ever married. They always seemed to be angry with one another. She felt lonely in her family and often wished for a normal mother and father.

Susan was responsible for putting her younger sister to bed at night after she had cleaned the kitchen of dishes from the evening meal. Susan knew her mother disapproved of her father's late nights out and did her best to help her mother with the household chores and her sister. Her mother rarely complimented her, and Susan constantly felt like she was never good enough, no matter how hard she tried to please her mother. Susan felt if she could just make her mother happy and proud of her, everything would be all right.

Susan was usually awake when her father came home. Sometimes he would rage and demand that the entire family wake up, get out of bed and meet him in the kitchen. Once everyone had assembled, he would complain about a bit of dust on the floor or the half-full garbage pail under the sink, or the few toys scattered about the house. On many occasions he would have Susan and her sister rewash the dinner dishes until he decided they were clean enough. Susan's mother never opposed his drunken rages, and Susan wondered if her mother was as frightened of him as she was.

One night he came home in an angry drunken rage and locked her mother out of the house. Susan felt scared, powerless and alone as she watched her mother get into the family car and drive away in the early morning hours.

Usually when Susan's father would have a tantrum in the middle of the night, she would imagine these two adults she lived with were not her real parents and that some day somebody would come and fix these two crazy, sick adults into the nice parents they were supposed to be.

Sometimes, Susan's father would push or even hit her mother, and Susan would be overwhelmed with a feeling of helplessness as she looked on, protecting her sister, wondering how she could rescue her mother from her pain. When her father would hit her she would make a conscious decision not to cry to prove to him he couldn't hurt her. Susan found it easier to be hit herself, as opposed to watching her mother or sister be abused, because she could survive by numbing her body.

At times Susan was afraid he would kill her mother and feared if this happened, she would be all alone and unprotected from her father's raging. What Susan did not realize was that with her mother there she was not protected and never had been protected. Her mother would stand paralyzed in a corner, not protecting herself or running from her father's blows. Susan watched her mother become a child while being abused and wished her mother would act like a grown-up who could protect her and her sister by putting a stop to her father's raging behavior. On several occasions she feared her father would even kill her.

Several times when Susan's father was drunk but not raging, he would come to her bedroom and crawl into her bed with her. During these times he would touch her on her genitals. She would freeze her body and pretend that she was asleep, hoping he would go away. She had nightmares about snakes and spiders hurting her and feared being alone in her bed at night. She tried to explain her fears to her mother, but was told to grow up and be a brave big girl for her little sister. Eventually Susan forgot how her father would touch her at night in the bed and discovered she could escape the feeling of his hands by talking silently with her imaginary friend. She and her sister would also play secret games with one another when her father was drunk and neither of her parents ever knew about these games.

Starting All Over Again

Susan ran away from home at the age of 17 and went to live with her boyfriend, Jay. She was relieved to be away from her parents and vowed to have a different life with Jay . . . full of love and happiness.

For the first year, living with Jay was a wonderful experience. But then things began to change. Jay and his friends would drink a lot together after work and Susan noticed that he became very critical of her after drinking. On several occasions he slapped her on the face and accused her of cheating on him. Susan was very faithful to Jay and tried to convince him of her commitment to him and the relationship.

After such episodes, on the following day, Jay would bring her flowers and tell her how sorry he was for his behavior the night before. For several years flowers and apologies were all that were necessary for Susan to feel content with her relationship with Jay and his abusive behavior while drinking. She really wanted her relationship with Jay to work out.

Eventually Jay's physically abusive behavior became more destructive, and on several occasions Susan ended up at her doctor's office with fractures and bruises. When her doctor would ask her about her injuries, she would lie to him, saying they were the result of a fall or a bump into a door.

Susan tried desperately to be a good mate to Jay, hoping her efforts would improve his treatment of her. She cooked all his favorite meals, brought home a respectable paycheck, was always available to him in the bedroom and more. She tried candlelight dinners, sexy nightwear and other surprises in order to please Jay, but nothing seemed to improve his behavior. At times, Susan felt like a failure as a mate and would wonder what she was doing wrong.

After a few years of living together, Susan and Jay decided things would improve if they married. Susan hoped marriage would calm Jay down, but the drinking and hitting increased. She left him several times, but would always return to him after he would vow never to drink or hit her again. After such incidents he would treat Susan to a trip to the Bahamas or to a new wardrobe, and Susan would feel as though they were starting all over again in their relationship. Each time Susan truly believed Jay's behavior was going to change for the better. Unfortunately the honeymoon would end after several months, with the drinking and abuse starting all over again

Susan eventually went to therapy to try to understand how her relationship with Jay could be *fixed*. While sharing with her therapist about her relationship with Jay, she noticed her therapist appeared very concerned for her well-being. When questioned about her responses to Jay's physically abusive behavior, Susan replied to her therapist it had been going on for so long, she was used to it. Her therapist seemed shocked with her reply and asked her why she was allowing herself to be abused, not leaving the situation and finding at least temporary safety for herself. Susan shared with her therapist that the hitting really wasn't that bad.

Understanding Repeat Behavior

As her therapist begins to educate Susan on what abusive behavior is, Susan begins to realize she and Jay are very sick and that their relationship is severely dysfunctional. She also realizes, to her dismay, she is repeating in her adult life those behaviors she witnessed in her mother while growing up. She begins to discover that as a result of her father's abusive behavior towards her, her sister and her mother, she has learned how to block out most of the physical and emotional pain inflicted upon her by Jay in her current situation. She begins to see that because she can block out her pain, she is continuing in an abusive relationship not realizing she is being severely violated. As she begins to learn about the many choices available to her in her relationship with Jay, she discovers that she hasn't any skills for implementing these changes.

During her therapy she role-plays confronting Jay and feels powerful and responsible after her session. But when attempting to confront Jay face to face, she becomes paralyzed with fear and feels as though she is a terrified five-year-old with her father raging at her.

When children are emotionally, physically or sexually abused, they are being disempowered and told verbally or nonverbally, "You haven't any rights. I, the adult, am in control of your destiny and life and you are powerless to do anything about it." The fear of being physically abandoned by major caretakers for not obeying their rules necessitates being quiet, not rocking the boat and otherwise not attempting to exercise personal power. In most situations, rebelling or exercising choice or self-care may promote more abuse, so children learn how to survive the abuse by blocking feelings of terror, rage, abandonment, grief and shame in any way possible.

Susan learned how to block out pain in response to her father's abusive behavior towards her during childhood. As she watched her mother accept violent blows and remarks from her father, she also learned she did not have a choice as to whether or not she could protect herself from the abuse of others. Her mother did not model healthy behavior for her to protect herself from the abuse and inappropriate behavior from others. Also Susan's mother did not protect her and, in essence, abandoned her to the rage of her father. Susan does not know how to protect herself in adult life with Jay as a consequence of not being protected in her youth. Also when Jay rages at her, she not only experiences the pain of the current abusive experience, but also re-experiences the terror of being abused in childhood. Using her childhood skills for numbing pain, she survives her current pain as she does her past pain.

Susan will need to begin experiencing all of her pain about the emotional, physical and sexual abuse she experienced in her family of origin to begin seeing how her current relationship parallels the abuse she grew up with. As she begins to experience her rage and grief over the trauma she endured during childhood, she also will begin to experience her rage and grief about her abusive relationship with Jay. When she begins expressing her feelings about being abused in childhood, healing begins. She will slowly discover her own personal power and realize she never deserved to be abused in the first place by her parents or Jay.

As her self-love and esteem increase, she will discover she is worth protecting and taking care of. Eventually Susan will even begin to remember how her father sexually abused her, along with the physical and emotional abuse, and will learn that as a result of this abuse, she was never able to develop the necessary skills for self-care and protection in adult life. With this information she will realize she was never offered choices in childhood and will learn that she now has a right to exercise choice in how she is treated by others.

One woman said to me, upon realizing she had a right to take care of herself, "I really can say no, can't I?" It was as if she had never considered the word *no* to be a part of her vocabulary until after entering recovery.

Children who are disempowered as a consequence of abuse have difficulty saying no to others and setting limits in adulthood for fear of being abandoned, rejected or abused by those they set limits with. They continue to be used, abused and victimized until the pain becomes intense enough to move them towards exploring the origins of their victim roles.

Putting Up With Abusive Behavior

After several years of recovery from alcohol, drug and food dependency, I became painfully aware of my most obvious dysfunctional survival skill from childhood. This particular survival skill perpetuated my role as a victim. I call this survival skill "putting up with abusive behavior from others." By putting up with the abusive behavior of others, not setting limits or taking care of myself in relationships, I continued to act out my role as a victim. There was a tremendous payoff for me in this role, and this payoff had originated in my childhood.

As mentioned earlier, I am a survivor of abuse and learned at an early age how to disassociate myself from the pain I experienced. Even in adulthood today, I will catch myself automatically numbing myself when confronted with offender behavior from others.

Many years back I was at a street dance. The dance was loads of fun and I really enjoyed myself. While walking home shoeless, Michael noticed I had a cut on my heel. I had automatically numbed my physical body when cut and was not even aware of my injury. In adulthood I continued to block emotional pain, just as I had the cut on my foot. People would use me materially and emotionally and I would be totally unaware of their motives. It was as if I were blind-sided and caught totally off guard. Later, after realizing I had been used, abused or taken advantage of once again, I would ask myself, "How did this happen?" Michael would look at me and sigh, "You should have personalized license plates that say, 'Hurt me, I'm a victim.'" I often wondered why I found myself in this type of situation over and over again.

Never Saying No — Always Saying Yes

Most of us come from families of origin where the option to say no to the demands of those adults around us was not available. As mentioned earlier, my son, Aaron's, favorite word at age two was, "No! No! No!" But for most of us, we heard directions from those adults around us like, "Don't talk back to your parents . . . Do as you are told with no questions asked . . . What I say goes, no matter what, because I am an adult." This stunted our exploration of the word *no*. In conjunction with our family of origin rules, we also learned another, which goes, "Never disobey your parents . . . Always listen to adults . . . Always do what you are told." In other words, always say yes without questioning, and even if you disagree with the request, no matter what, do it anyway.

As adults we end up saying yes to virtually all requests and rarely say no to even the most ludicrous demands. We end up feeling used, abused and unappreciated. Some of us are abused emotionally by our friends, mates and even our children, feeling powerless in caring for ourselves in such situations.

I have worked with mothers who are themselves survivors of abuse whose main complaint when visiting my office is, "I don't know how to set limits and say no to my children. They don't listen to me and are even at times emotionally abusive. I always seem to give in too easily."

Many parents share that they have difficulty following through on disciplinary consequences to the inappropriate behavior of their children. They may threaten with consequences but not follow through or they may begin to initiate disciplinary actions only to revoke them at the pleas of their children.

Others can never say no to a mate or spouse, even to sexual activities which seem uncomfortable or, in some situations, distasteful.

Workmates pile extra work on us and we have difficulty denying them. Relatives drop in on us unexpectedly for dinner or overnight and we quietly accommodate them, never knowing we have the right to say no instead of yes.

Recently while in Wales, I was talking with a young recovering Welsh alcoholic man. He was very upset because several of his relatives from England had ". . . popped in unannounced to spend the night." He also shared that they drank quite a bit and, being new in recovery, their sudden visit made him nervous. While sharing this, he talked as if he hadn't any options to his dilemma. The word *no* was not a choice for this man. He was resigned to put up with his drunken relatives as best as possible. I suggested the option "No" and he appeared completely surprised, not having even thought of it.

Children who are disempowered during trauma grow into adults who feel powerless in making choices and decisions for their own well-being. They continue to accept the abuse and boundary violation from others as they did in childhood, not knowing they have a right to say, "No, I won't allow you to hurt me . . . No, I can't accept that kind of behavior from you . . . Your remark about me is offensive . . . I will not be responsible for your personal difficulties in life . . . Your addictive behavior is inappropriate and abusive to me . . . I am offended by your behavior."

Periodically I work with individuals who are in severely dysfunctional relationships. Usually they come to therapy in pain about the relationship, looking for solutions to quickly resolve the difficulties. In some situations, these individuals are involved with mates who are emotionally, physically and/or even sexually abusive.

TOM AND LINDA'S STORY Tom, for instance, married Linda at a very early age. He and Linda were high school sweethearts and it seemed only natural for them to marry. Tom loved Linda with all of his heart and worked hard to be a good provider for her, just as his father had done for his mother.

Tom's parents had been concerned when Tom married Linda because they knew she had a bit of a drinking problem. Both Tom's parents had grown up in families where alcohol was often overused and abused so each knew about living with alcoholism. Tom had never seen his parents drink alcohol, except now and then on special occasions or during the holiday seasons. They never kept liquor in the house and gave away presents of bottled liquor which were given to them. Both of Tom's parents feared what lay ahead for their son in his relationship with Linda.

Initially Tom was very happy in his relationship with his wife. He was aware of her drinking habits, but was not concerned. He had watched his uncles drink and get drunk for many years and knew Linda didn't drink like that.

Linda was an attractive woman and on the job she received a great deal of attention from her male peers. She enjoyed the compliments and especially appreciated the attention she received from one particular male colleague. Linda and Bill would have lunch and break-time together. After a while Linda and Bill began having a sexual relationship.

Tom knew something was different about Linda because she was distancing herself from him, both emotionally and physically. Several of Tom's friends shared their concerns about Linda's relationship with her colleague, but Tom had difficulty accepting what he was hearing. He even discussed his concerns with Linda. Linda denied being unfaithful and told Tom she was angry that he would even accuse her. Tom dropped the issue, feeling ashamed for even bringing it up.

Linda had continued her affair while her drinking progressed. Linda knew something was wrong with her drinking but vowed to Tom she would be more cautious after each incident of overindulging. When at friends' homes or gatherings with relatives, Linda would periodically become morose and depressed after several drinks. Tom would apologize to his hosts for her behavior as he escorted her out to the car and home to bed.

Tom was embarrassed by comments made about Linda by family or friends and was always quick to defend her behavior. Linda would apologize to Tom and tell him if it wasn't for his strength, she wouldn't know how to survive. Tom believed he was truly responsible for Linda's welfare and at times felt the burden of this responsibility was more than he could bear.

Tom began to hear a number of comments about Linda's relationship with a man at her work. He heard they were meeting for lunch together and were very friendly with one another.

One day Tom decided to follow Linda during lunch and, much to his dismay, discovered his friends' observations were much more than rumors. He confronted Linda that evening. She told him she was very sorry, but she felt he did not give her the love she needed. Linda also shared if he had paid more attention to her, she would not have found it necessary to look outside of her marriage for love. Tom felt totally confused because he had confronted Linda about the affair and now she was blaming it on him. He asked himself, "Am I really responsible?"

Tom has difficulty asserting and protecting himself in his relationship with Linda because he is a second generation adult child of an alcoholic. Both of his parents grew up in chaotic, abusive alcoholic families where neither of them learned how to set healthy limits or boundaries with others or for themselves. While raising Tom, their need for structure set Tom up to be very rigid. Tom rarely saw either of his parents express themselves and never saw them argue. When he met Linda, he was refreshed by the way in which she expressed herself and at times was even envious. Tom does not know how to trust himself, his perceptions or feelings and is more prone to trust the perceptions of others.

Trusting Our Perceptions

When we cannot trust our own perceptions of what we feel, hear or see, we will not be able to establish healthy boundaries. Each of us has the gift of intuition which gives us clues to our environment. When we grow up in chaotic families, we discover it is not safe for us to trust our perceptions of what we hear, see or feel. Children learn how to trust themselves by being validated by their parents.

While growing up in my family of origin, I knew something was terribly wrong. People acted funny, especially when they drank, and I would ask other family members, "Doesn't something seem wrong here?" Their reply would be, "How could you say such a thing? You have an overactive imagination."

Recently I was addressing some unfinished family of origin business for my own personal growth. I had some missing pieces to a part of my past and phoned a family friend for some possible clues that would hopefully complete the picture. When I shared what I had discovered, he immediately told me to leave the issue alone, that it wasn't that important. He also suggested I was making a mountain out of a molehill. I felt at that moment as I had during childhood. I felt shamed, confused and began discounting the information I had discovered. For a split second I thought, "Maybe I am making a mountain out of a molehill." At that moment, I had lost my reality, my boundaries and myself. I was once again believing the reality of another over my own. My healthy self immediately yelled, "Carla, where are your boundaries? You're being shamed and discounted. Take care of yourself." My intuition said, "Please don't block me out after we have worked so hard to reach this point. Trust me! You're not making a mountain out of a molehill. This is serious."

We must learn how to trust our own intuition before we can have healthy relationships with others. We have all heard the saying "Don't judge a book by its cover." In some life experiences this may apply, but in other situations, our first strong impression of a situation is our intuitive self saying, "Open your eyes and beware . . .

Something isn't right . . . You'd better take responsibility for yourself." Once we trust our intuition, we can be safe in most situations with most people.

Tom is more willing to trust Linda's perceptions than his own. This is a red flag indicator of his lack of healthy boundaries. He knew something was wrong because initially he felt her distancing emotionally and physically. He even had healthy validation of his feelings from friends and relatives. And to top it off, Tom witnessed Linda's addictive behavior with her office mate with his very own eyes. But Tom never learned to trust himself because his parents were not able to provide him with the tools necessary to do so, due to their own unresolved childhood issues.

The disempowered victim feels powerless in the area of self-trust. Also, as Janet Woititz has pointed out, adult children of alcoholics tend to be loyal, even when that loyalty is not deserved. I believe this not only applies to adult children of alcoholics, but to anyone who comes from a dysfunctional family, whether the dysfunction is a consequence of behavioral addiction, such as work or sex addiction, etc., or any other family stressor.

Our responsibility is to explore how we were originally disempowered. Once we make this discovery, we must have our feelings about our loss and pain and then heal from our youth. As we heal, we will learn that as children we were victimized unknowingly, and in some cases knowingly, by our caretakers. As we discover the origins of our disempowerment, we will be able to begin making choices as to whether or not we will continue being victimized as we were during childhood. By allowing ourselves to heal from the traumas of youth, we are taking adult responsibility not only for our well-being, but also for our existence. By learning how to be responsible for ourselves, we also begin to appreciate our successes and triumphs in life. By exploring our families of origin, healing from our childhood pain and accepting adult responsibility for ourselves, we are freed from the restrictive scripts of the past.

The Victim In
Recovery

6

When I finally began finding solutions to my addictive behavior, I thought I had found Utopia. I truly believed all my relationship difficulties would be straightened out and life would be blissfully peaceful. I went from one mode of deluded thinking to another with expectations of kindness from all now that I was addressing my addictions. More specifically, I expected that those recovering from addiction who were like myself would be devoid of all offensive characteristics.

In other words, I walked into recovery with blinders on and carried with me a fantasy about how recovering people should behave.

My first several years of recovery were wonderful because I felt for the first time in my life that I was with groups of people who were just like me. It was a relief to know there were others who had drunk Nyquil, binged on popcorn and felt totally washed up as human beings. I was willing to do anything to be accepted by these groups and was also willing to "go to any lengths," as they say, to avoid returning to my self-destructive behavior. But unfortunately going to any lengths in my case involved not having any boundaries and recreating my dysfunctional family of origin within recovery groups.

For those first several years in recovery I allowed myself to be used emotionally and financially and was abused verbally and spiritually. This is not to say that all people in recovery programs are offenders. What does need to be said is that I, as an individual without any boundaries in early recovery, continued to attract to myself others in recovery programs who did have offender characteristics.

Addiction of any kind covers up the pain, shame and fear addicts have about their behavior and unresolved past and current relationships. When the addiction is removed — whether that addiction is alcoholism, drug addiction, eating addiction, work addiction, sexual addiction, shopping addiction, gambling addiction, religious addiction, people addiction, etc. — the behaviors, fears and problems addiction covered up are still alive and well. I truly believed that if I abstained from my addictive behavior, I would immediately heal from my victim role. Not only did it take time to recover from my lack of boundaries, but being victimized sober was much more painful than while under the influence of booze, pills or food. As I still had victim characteristics, I sought out offenders abstaining from alcohol, drugs, food, sex, etc., who had offender characteristics which were not only apparent before their recovery, but also after abstaining from addiction.

I found myself giving people money I couldn't afford, not knowing I had the choice to say no. I would spend four to five hours per day listening to the suffering of another addict, not realizing I needed to set limits. I would chauffeur, cook and even clean for other addicts, believing this was my lot in recovery — to do, do, do for others while feeling resentful, used and abused. Then I would feel shame for my feelings of anger towards these people who, like me, were trying to recover from addiction.

Repeating The Familiar

The majority of my women friends in early recovery had many characteristics similar to my mother and I found myself responding to them as I had with my mother in childhood. I felt emotionally abandoned, discounted and rejected with these women and could not understand what it was I was doing in these relationships that caused me such intense pain. I also attracted a number of male offenders who were inappropriate in behavior, and I began fearing certain recovery groups. I thought to myself, "If this is what recovery is, I don't want it."

I wanted to hide out, feeling abused, until one day I was given a gift. A recovering alcoholic, food addict, sexual abuse survivor said to me, "Carla, your 'friend picker' is real sick. You seek out people who will hurt you." Well — Surprise! Surprise! — this was news to me. But I still did not know how to distinguish a safe versus a potentially abusive relationship. In other words, I needed a warning system that would clue me in to possible unsafe situations. I needed to be responsible but had absolutely no awareness of offender behavior from others until after the fact.

When being offended, I would numb out and discount my perceptions of the situation as it really was, just as I had learned to do in childhood. After the fact, I would feel stupid and inadequate, wondering once again what I had done to place myself in such a situation. I kept hearing a voice inside of me say, "Carla, take care of yourself! You're responsible for you." I knew how to take care of others and give myself to anybody but I didn't know how to protect myself.

One day I became really frustrated as I watched my young son at play with one of his friends. His friend was trying to take a toy away from him and Aaron was saying, "No! That's mine!" I thought, "Now, why can't I do that?"

CHRIS' STORY | Chris had been in recovery for her alcoholism for several years and had done a great deal of family of origin work on herself. She had discovered that her father was an alcoholic and that her mother basically ran the household while she was growing up. She never really knew her father had a drinking problem until she went to an alcohol awareness class to learn more about her own disease.

When Chris would drink, she would become loud and the life of any party. She never really believed her father was alcoholic because she had never seen him drunk and all he ever drank was a few beers each day after work. Chris learned not only about her own alcoholism, but also how her father's alcoholism had affected her. She also learned that her mother's behavior had had a big effect on her while she was growing up. In fact she began to realize that although her mother didn't drink, her behavior was still very dysfunctional.

Chris discovered her father was emotionally unavailable because his life revolved around his alcoholism, and her mother had emotionally abandoned her because her mother's life rotated around her father and his drinking.

Chris had always thought her family was normal and that she was the one disgrace because of her alcoholism. The myth of her family was further shattered when she began to realize she had been severely emotionally abused. Chris had never considered herself to be a victim of abuse because neither parent had ever hit her. She was shocked to learn that the type of abuse she had suffered was just as damaging as physical abuse.

Triangulating: The Go-Between

While growing up, she would listen to her mother's complaints about her father on a regular basis. At times her mother would have her relay messages to her father, such as, "Tell your father to quit making so much noise in the garage" or "Tell your father we are going to eat without him if he doesn't come inside now." Chris' mother would also share with her those angry feelings she had towards her father. "Your father is so lazy . . . Your father really doesn't care about us."

When she spent time with her father, he would ask, "Do you know what is wrong with your mother? I can't understand why she behaves the way she does." In order to ease her father's confusion, she would share with him some of the complaints her mother had.

After visiting with her father in the garage and returning to the house, her mother would ask, "What's he had to say and why is he staying out in that garage for so long?" Chris felt like a ping-pong ball being bounced back and forth between her parents. As an adult, her parents continued to involve her in their disputes. Chris felt as though she was fighting their battles for them and wished they would just settle their differences between themselves.

Upon entering recovery for her alcoholism, Chris made a number of friends. She had two very close friends whom she loved dearly, but there was a problem. The two of them disliked one another and would make comments to her about each other on a regular basis.

While in her early years of recovery, she began to learn about a dysfunctional family-system process called triangulation. She learned that her parents had triangulated her into their relationship and made her the go-between so that they would never have to directly confront one another. The payoff for being the go-between for her parents was receiving the attention she so desperately craved from them, even though it was abusive and dysfunctional. She also learned that by being placed in the middle of her parents' problems, she felt important, needed, loved and as though she had a place in the family. Chris had always feared she would just disappear from not being noticed by her parents and learned she could make her presence known by being in the thick of it when her parents needed her as the go-between.

The price for this family role caused Chris a great deal of pain. There were times during her youth when she would be at the receiving end of the angry feelings her parents had for one another. Her mother would be angry with her for not relaying the messages correctly or her father would ignore her if he disliked the message she was relaying to him from her mother.

One day her father blew up in the garage after she shared with him what her mother had said. Chris was scared as she watched her father rage and felt as though she had done something wrong.

It is abusive to set children up to be message carriers between two adults. The child's emotional welfare is being ignored during such times, and the child is being abandoned. The needs of the adults are being served at the expense of the child, so the child learns to get his or her need for attention fulfilled by becoming involved in the problems of others. In adulthood, children such as this grow into individuals who constantly find themselves involved in the problems of others. They are the buffers for those individuals who have difficulty with confrontation, and being the buffers, they absorb pain, anger and other feelings which aren't supposed to be for them. Their payoff is to be needed and not abandoned. Although they may initially feel useful and accepted in situations such as this, in reality they are being used, abused and emotionally abandoned. Their friendships are based on their position as buffer and they repeat this family of origin pattern in adulthood.

Back to our scenario of Chris and her two friends who dislike each other, Chris begins to realize that each of these friends is giving her information to take back to the other. She feels used and hurt and realizes neither are really interested in her feelings, that the two of them need to talk with one another, instead of using her as the messenger. She also begins to see that she is repeating a pattern from childhood and feels anger at her parents for establishing this way of relating.

Many come to my office with concerns about relationships in recovery. Like Chris and myself, they find themselves recreating their family of origin within recovery support groups. Their expectations are that this should not be happening with friends who are working on themselves and their addictions. They lose faith in the recovery process, their friends in recovery and themselves. Few realize at the beginning that it is up to them to find out where the dysfunctional relationship patterns originated.

ANDY'S STORY | Andy has been in recovery from his workaholism and eating disorder for several years. He has successfully abstained from overworking and overeating for

Figure 6.1. Unhealthy Communication

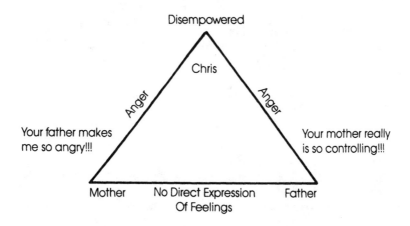

Figure 6.2. Chris Receiving Anger That Isn't Hers

Direct Communication And Expression Of Feelings

Mother --- Father

I'm angry at you when _____
you come home late

I'm angry with your _____
drinking

_____ I'm angry with your
nagging

_____ I'm angry with your
controlling behavior

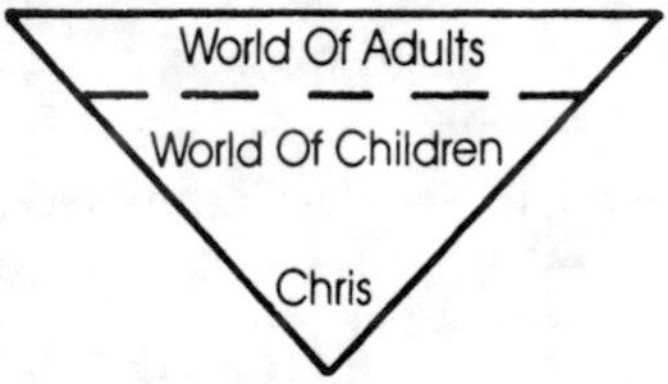

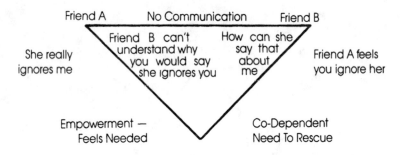

World Of Adults

World Of Children

Chris

Figure 6.3. Healthy Communication

Friend A   No Communication   Friend B

She really   Friend B can't   How can she   Friend A feels
ignores me   understand why   say that   you ignore her
                    you would say   about
                    she ignores you   me

Empowerment —   Co-Dependent
Feels Needed   Need To Rescue

Chris feels needed by both of her friends in this situation. But she is enabling them to not settle their differences directly and cannot have an intimate relationship with either because she is being used and abused. The abuse may not be a conscious motive on the part of her friends, but it is abusive none the less.

Figure 6.4. Unhealthy Friendship

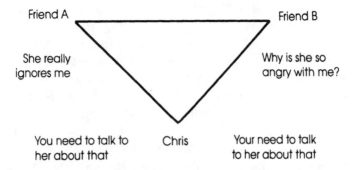

Friend A   Friend B

She really   Why is she so
ignores me   angry with me?

You need to talk to   Chris   Your need to talk
her about that   to her about that

Chris needs to pull out of the middle of the triangle. She may anger Friend A or Friend B or both, but for her own recovery and establishment of her boundaries, she must give up the role as the go-between. In order for her to experience healthy intimate relationships, Chris must learn healthy relationships involve open communication all the way around.

Figure 6.5. Healthy Friendship

quite a while but is still unhappy with his male and female friendships. When he entered recovery and began working on himself, he started having real male friends for the first time in his life. Before recovery, his relationships with other males were superficial and limited to discussions of sports and work. In his relationships in recovery, he talks with other men about his feelings.

Learning From Our Same-Sexed Parent

He does find one consistent pattern in his relationship with men which causes him difficulty. The men he has the closest relationships with always eventually want to run his life, just as his father did. They begin telling him what he should do and what he is doing wrong. Andy becomes resentful of their advice, wishing not for another father figure, but for a friend. When he confronts these father figures on their behavior, surprisingly they react to him as his own father would — with resentment and anger. Andy then feels powerless and shamed, as he so often felt with his father while growing up.

Andy never felt he was successful enough for his father and always felt his father's expectations of him were more than he could achieve. He carried this belief on into adulthood, feeling as though he was lacking somewhere deep inside himself, never able to feel complete. He had always wanted his father's approval and had worked hard to get it, but his father always criticized him, no matter how accomplished he was. Andy could not remember a time when his father did not believe some part of his life was in need of improvement. Andy had reached a point where he didn't share his life with his father anymore because he was tired of his father's need to advise him on how to improve himself.

Repeating The Familiar

Initially he was excited to find a group of recovering men to spend time with and felt very safe with several of them in particular. Andy believed he was finally experiencing some healthy male relationships until he began feeling resentment about some of the advice given from his friends. He did not know how to express his resentment about the advice-giving and decided it would be easier to just drop out of the group.

Eventually he found a new group of recovering men and began to feel very at home in their company. But eventually and inevitably several of the older men began giving him advice, and he found himself abandoning yet another group.

He began to wonder why his friends always found it necessary to constantly want to give him advice. It angered him and he felt trapped once they began telling him what in his life needed changing. They made him feel inadequate and not as competent as his other men friends. It was as if Andy surrounded himself with men who were like his father, even though he thought he went out of his way to avoid men he saw as having those characteristics.

Andy's first experience with a male came from his relationship with his father who was rigid, demanding and perfectionistic. When Andy's father continually criticized him during his youth, he was disempowering Andy, not providing him with a sense of self-worth as a man.

Andy continues to unconsciously seek out the familiar in his men's groups. He has a frozen need for fathering because his father didn't provide healthy fathering for him. Unconsciously he seeks out those familiar characteristics of his father's in others in response to the lack of nurturing from his father in childhood. It is as if there is a part of him still looking for a father who will fulfill those frozen needs for the nurturing he still desperately craves.

When one of his male friends gives him advice, he feels inadequate and disempowered again, as he was by his father, not able to separate his friend's suggestions from his father's criticisms. At this point, Andy does not know he has the right to set limits with those who choose to offer advice. As a child he was never given a choice or option, but was always expected to follow his father's rigid will.

In order for Andy to begin exercising his boundaries and set limits with those who give him advice, he will need to resolve the pain, rage and shame he has about his father's lack of encouragement and excessive demand for perfection. By having his feelings about his relationship with his father, Andy will be able to reclaim his power as a grown man and be able to separate his concept of his father from his men friends. He will learn that not all advice-giving males are like his father and that he has a right to say, "Thanks, but no thanks."

Andy will learn that he has to become his own best friend and parent. He will have to grieve the losses he experienced with his father. As Andy learns it is his responsibility to fulfill his own needs, he will discontinue his unconscious, or possibly conscious, search for a surrogate father. He will feel comfortable confronting older men and feel competent around not only older men friends, but also his father.

I had to grieve my relationship with my mother and explore those unresolved issues which were affecting me in my current relationship with women. As I did this, it was as if the blinders came off and the lights went on. For successful same-sexed relationships it is important for us to explore our relationship with our same-sexed parent and resolve those issues which affect us today.

Andy also experiences difficulties in his opposite-sexed relationship and as a result has been married three times. After his last relationship ended, he vowed to just play the field for a while, but soon found himself in another committed relationship.

His relationships always began sexually. Andy would find himself attracted to a female and would pursue her until they had sex. After they had sex, the excitement in the relationship would be gone. It was as if sex was the challenge and after the challenge was gone, the relationship felt empty. He would continue the relationship, feeling trapped and eventually resentful towards his mate. He had difficulty expressing his feelings, while each of his partners would rage about his lack of attention to them. Andy felt powerless to deal with their requests and deserving of their raging behavior. When he was raged at, he would shut down emotionally and withdraw. In each of his relationships, sex became the only method of connecting with females, and true intimacy was nonexistent. When the relationship ended, it was because his female partner had decided she wanted out. Andy would feel relieved. It was as if a weight had been lifted off his shoulders. Several times during committed relationships, Andy had short-term affairs. As with his other relationships, after a sexual relationship had been achieved, the excitement would be gone.

Even in recovery, Andy was experiencing the same pattern in his relationships. Now in another committed relationship with Carol, he finds the excitement has again evaporated after having sex with her. He really likes and admires Carol and can't understand why he is losing interest. The only way Andy knows how to connect with a female is sexually, so he is totally incapable of experiencing true, honest communication or intimacy.

Andy's mother was a rageaholic. When she became angry, she would scream and yell. Andy never felt safe with her and withdrew into himself to survive the pain of her behavior. He learned that women are not safe from growing up with a mother who was a hostile rageaholic.

Andy's father was also demanding of his mother, who would respond to his criticisms by raising her voice and cursing him. Andy watched his father tune her out as if she were not there. This would infuriate his mother even more and her raging behavior would intensify. Andy learned to avoid the conflict between the two of them by escaping within himself.

As he grew older, he discovered masturbation and learned he could change the way he felt by masturbating. When his parents would fight, he would go to his room with a *Playboy* magazine and escape into fantasy. He felt safe with his magazines because they did not talk back, yell at him or make demands on him.

Andy has never learned how to have a healthy intimate relationship with a woman. His mother did not provide the safety to encourage him to explore interacting emotionally with a female in a healthy way. We learn about opposite-sexed relationships by interacting with our opposite-sexed parent. If our opposite-sexed parent is dysfunctional and/or abusive, we will develop a specific set of survival skills to allow us safety in that relationship. Although these survival skills will protect us in childhood, they will cause us difficulty in adulthood.

Andy has learned how to withdraw from conflict by tuning out his partners during times of conflict. As long as he is tuning out his mates he cannot experience true intimacy. When his mother raged at him, she disempowered him with emotional abuse. By raging at him, she taught him that angry women were to be feared. As an adult male he fears the anger of women and withdraws from them when they have anger or conflict with him. He does not know how to care for himself when confronted with anger. Also because his parents weren't able to resolve their own difficulties, Andy does not have the skills to resolve conflict. In other words, he doesn't know how to fight in a healthy manner.

Andy is also a sex addict who uses sex to escape those feelings he has difficulty with. He uses masturbation and fantasy to escape the turmoil of everyday life and uses sex in his relationships to repair feelings of conflict and pain. His problems are never resolved, only temporarily buried.

To learn how to experience all of his feelings, Andy will need to begin participating in a recovery program for sexual addiction. He also has a great deal of unfinished business with his mother which must be resolved for him to reclaim his right to his anger. Andy's mother set him up to not express feelings of anger by intimidating him with her raging behavior. As Andy learns how to have his feelings, he will begin to feel empowered and realize he does not have to run from anger. He will also learn the difference between the unhealthy offensive raging behavior his mother displayed and the healing empowering feelings of healthy anger he must experience for his recovery and growth.

Sex Addicts Anonymous

Andy starts attending Sex Addicts Anonymous, along with his other 12-Step programs, and begins to work in therapy on his unresolved issues involving his parents.

He learns that his addiction to nicotine has also allowed him to avoid his feelings. Nicotine is a drug and suppresses feelings of anger and fear. It is difficult to do effective family of origin work while under the influence of nicotine. Those I work with must not only be alcohol and drug free, but if they smoke or chew tobacco, they are required to abstain for one hour before their therapy session.

By attending S.A.A., Andy learns he uses sex and fantasy to avoid his feelings, so he begins to work an abstinence program which involves not using sex to escape his feeling. He and Carol decide to stick out the relationship and not run away from one another. They both decide if they do not work out their differences in this relationship, their problems will only follow them to the next and then the next and so on.

While working on his relationship with Carol, Andy learns how to fight with her and stand up for himself. Healthy fighting is necessary because during conflict we clear the air with one another and re-establish our boundaries.

Without recovery, most of us fight the way one of our parents did. Usually our parents' methods of fighting were unhealthy. It is important for us to learn how to express our anger towards one another in healthy ways, which means not allowing anybody to invade our boundaries with abusive behavior, while at the same time, not abusing the boundaries of the person we are in conflict with.

Healthy Fighting Rules

1. *No threats of abandonment to achieve control.* "Well, I guess our friendship ends here . . . We will just have to break off our relationship . . . Well, let's just get a divorce" are statements which sabotage healthy fighting. Once we are threatened or we threaten others with abandonment, it is difficult to continue communication. The party being threatened with abandonment fears being totally rejected and discontinues sharing at an honest level. Using the threat of abandonment as a weapon while fighting, destroys intimacy, possible resolution of conflict and trust. It is appropriate to ask for space and distance if one or both parties find themselves at an impasse, but threats of abandonment to achieve control are only a temporary solution.

2. *Fight about one thing at a time.* "Well, last week your behavior really was the pits . . . Remember several years ago at Christmas time . . . When I first met you, you did something to me that really hurt."

    Some of us have difficulty focusing on one issue at a time, especially if we feel unresolved about past issues. With "stringing," the issue at hand is never resolved because past issues are brought up as weapons to prove how injured each party has been in the relationship. When there are several unresolved issues being discussed at one time, it is difficult to resolve any of them. Learning how to fight in a healthy manner begins with staying focused on the issue which started the conflict. If there are past unresolved issues, those each need to be addressed one at a time and they need to be given appropriate time for resolution.

3. *No self-degrading behavior while fighting.* "Well, I really am just a rotten friend . . . I'm horrible and no good as a partner . . . I am a son of a bitch and a low life." "How can I fight with him when he is already so down?" is the thought which comes to mind when presented with one of the above statements. The tables turn away from the issue in dispute to repairing the self-esteem of the partner who is degrading self. "No, you're not really that bad." The conflict is not resolved, but pushed aside.

To degrade self during an argument sabotages resolution of the argument. When disagreements are not resolved, they will only emerge at a different time, in a different situation, to be addressed all over again. Self-degrading behavior while arguing displays a real lack of healthy boundaries.

4. *No physical or emotional violence.* "You no good f#@*!!! . . . You're just a b#@*!! like all other women . . . You're as crazy as a loon, you should be locked up . . . Keep it up and I'll slap you across the room." All of the above stop true, honest communication because they intimidate. When shaming and intimidation are used during conflict, the issues being discussed are no longer the focus of attention. The focus is on threats, shaming statements and at times on survival. When there is any form of physical pushing, shoving or hitting in a relationship, both partners are in need of serious help. When there is emotional abuse as a consequence of raging, belittling, name-calling or emotional withdrawal, professional help is strongly indi-

cated. To have healthy communication, the above behaviors must be eliminated.

5. *No shaming the other person for their feelings or perceptions.* "You don't know what you are talking about . . . How dare you bring this up . . . You don't really feel that way . . . You're just imagining that." To tell another person their feelings are wrong is inappropriate. We do not have to agree with another's perceptions or feelings, but it is important to respect them. So many of us believe a fight is resolved if we can get others to see it our way. Resolution involves allowing each person their perceptions and feelings about the situation at hand. It is not our job to convince them to agree with us, nor are we required to give up our feelings to make another feel comfortable. To be shamed or degraded for values, beliefs or feelings can shut down communication, and then resolution of conflict is impossible. Healthy intimacy is nonexistent and trust is lost.

6. *It's okay to take space.* "We are going to talk this thing out until it is resolved . . . I'm not hanging up the phone until we have this issue cleared up . . . You will not leave this room until we have finished . . . Nobody goes to bed, even if we have to stay up all night." Sometimes it's not possible to resolve a conflict in one space of time. Breaks are necessary and even encouraged. Taking time out allows both parties the space to re-evaluate the conflict at hand. Not communicating for a set amount of time can disenmesh the two parties enough to make the complicated incredibly clear. To insist that an issue be resolved when at an impasse, or when one or both parties are frustrated and tired, is counterproductive. Getting a fresh start after some distance can facilitate smooth resolution.

7. *Listen to one another.* Have you ever felt the person you were communicating with wasn't really listening to you? If you have, probably you were not being heard. We all talk to one another, but not everybody listens. Listening is very important, especially while fighting.

It is important for each person in the conflict to receive their share of talking time without interruption from the other. To talk over somebody else or to drown out another with a raised voice shows a real need to win.

Conflict resolution is not about winning, it's about listening to another's perceptions and feelings and then sharing our own. That's all conflict resolution involves. When we listen to another, we do not have to accept what they say, but it is important to hear where they are coming from. We also need to be listened to. Many conflicts are based on not listening. How often have you been accused of saying something and you say to yourself, "I don't remember saying that" or "I didn't mean for it to come out that way." Knowing how to listen is at the core of healthy intimacy.

Knowing how to fight allows us to clear up miscommunications and violated boundaries. Healthy fighting can build trust and free up a stale relationship of old unresolved resentments. Learning how to fight in recovery is one of the keys to learning how to have healthy boundaries. Those who really care about one another can give each other a great gift during times of disagreement. That gift is the gift of healthy confrontation, which says, "I value our relationship enough to let you know how I really feel."

Building boundaries in recovery can be frustrating and painful because we are learning in adulthood what young children learn today. But when we begin the painful process of saying, "No, I can't do that for you . . . I need to take care of myself . . . I'm angry with your behavior . . . I find that remark offensive," we will slowly see how capable we really are at taking care of ourselves.

No longer will we be afraid of life, but wish to embrace it with all its risks, joys and even pains. Life is to be experienced, and with healthy boundaries we no longer need to hide out, fearing victimization. We can become a part of life, living it to the fullest.

The Overempowered Individual | 7

I believe it is important for all of us to have a sense of empowerment so that we are able to take care of ourselves in healthy ways. It is important for children to develop a healthy sense of empowerment. This comes from tackling childhood frustrations and succeeding.

Back to my son Aaron — when he was about two years old, Michael and I bought him a bike with training wheels. Initially he had difficulty pedaling and quickly became frustrated. He would cry and kick and eventually ask Mama for a push. This went on for about six months, and at times, being co-dependent, I would cringe while Aaron would scream in frustration at the top of his lungs. I feared the neighbors' reactions, but I knew Aaron needed to experience his frustration for his growth.

Eventually Aaron mastered pedaling his bike. Success was written all over his face. Aaron had mastered what initially seemed impossible, but through this experience he was able to feel his own power. Mama no longer needed to give him a push because through his frustration he had been empowered and learned he could succeed on his own merit.

Learning From Frustration

Frustration is necessasry for a child's development of self-esteem and mastery. Frustration forces children to grow and teaches us how to take care of ourselves in adulthood. If children are not frustrated, they cannot learn about challenge. If life's experiences in childhood are too easy, they will not know how to cope with the difficulties of adulthood.

Many parents do, do, do for their children when they sense their child's frustration. By doing this they are disempowering their child and not allowing him or her to grow, succeed and experience their own sense of power.

At the same time these parents are also overempowering their children by placing the child's needs above their own. This teaches children that life really does rotate around them and that they really are the center of the universe.

Children like this grow into adults who lack those skills necessary for self-sufficiency. They believe their needs are more important than those of others and also expect others to fulfill them. Some refer to children such as this as spoiled brats. They appear to be overindulged, and are very common in families which seem to be functional but in reality are extremely dysfunctional.

Parents in such family systems have several characteristics in common. One of the most prevalent characteristics is that of not wanting to do to their children what was done to them. Usually the parents come from extremely dysfunctional family systems, and in many cases are survivors of emotional, spiritual, physical or sexual abuse. During their childhoods the abuse they endured was disempowering so they swing 180 degrees in the opposite direction, producing a generation of overempowered children.

One of the most common family systems producing overempowered children comes from those parents who are in recovery for addiction and/or their family of origin issues.

SANDY'S STORY | Sandy has been in recovery for her alcoholism for three years. She divorced her cocaine-addicted husband when he refused to get help for his addiction. Sandy was raised with an alcoholic father and a very co-dependent mother. Her father would rage periodically and frighten Sandy. Her mother constantly criticized her during her youth and she never felt she could please her. Sandy's mother still criticizes her, especially regarding her parenting skills with her daughter, Lilly. Sandy's mother tells her that she is spoiling her child rotten and that what Lilly needs is a good spanking. Sandy feels torn because she is painfully aware of how demanding and hostile her five-year-old daughter is. But Sandy does not want to discipline her daughter as her mother disciplined her.

When Sandy was small, discipline came in the form of swats with belts and coat hangers on her behind. She remembers learning at a very early age to stuff her feelings, even though the physical and emotional pain were intense. She knew to keep quiet and felt intimidated and scared of her father's rage.

As a recovering alcoholic, Sandy realizes she, too, has a raging problem. Before recovery she could bury her rage with alcohol, but now in recovery, her rage can be overwhelming. She fears her rage and has concerns about its effect on her daughter. As Sandy is not in touch with her anger when it arises, she automatically and unconsciously stuffs it. After stuffing her emotions over several instances of anger, anything can trigger it all back at one time. When it all surfaces at once, it is no longer anger, it's rage. (See Figure 7.1.)

Most ragers are not aware their raging is about a great deal of stuffed past and present anger, even though those around them are aware that their reaction is excessive in relation to the issue at hand. Also when feeling trapped or out of control of a situation, rage is easily triggered for the rageaholic. When feeling trapped or out of control or when there is an overwhelming sense of frustration, shame or failure, raging temporarily places the rager back in control. Raging displaces feelings of disempowerment with feelings

Rage is addictive.
Rage is overwhelming.
Rage is scary.
Rage is uncontrollable.
Rage is fear-inducing to those around.
Rage is an unhealthy boundary.

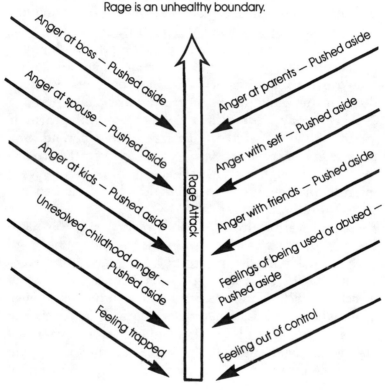

Initial reaction to incident in the here and now which triggers all the
    stuffed rage, such as . . .
Dishwater not emptied
Bed not made
Negative comment from friend, relative or spouse.

Figure 7.1. The Process Of A Rage Attack

of overempowerment and control. Individuals who rage have been disempowered in childhood and find that raging gives them a renewed sense of strength. This quest for power produces the addiction of rageaholism, which is an inappropriate expression of anger that is offensive and usually misdirected. When children are raised with rageaholics and/or abused, they are at risk for raging also. They may rage outwardly or they may rage inwardly, both of which are dysfunctional. By raging outwardly, individuals feeling unsafe, trapped, frustrated or out of control produce a false sense of security with a barrier of verbal and, in some cases, physical rage. This barrier of rage proclaims, "I need control." By raging inwardly, that is by stuffing their rage, those in the rager's environment "walk on eggshells," trying not to rock the boat or push the rager into raging outwardly. Once again the rager has established a barrier which says, "Don't upset me or else . . ., placing themselves in control. Everyone knows the rager is rageful, so they conform and caretake to keep the rager from exploding."

Rageaholism impacts young children and, in Sandy's case, her raging behavior is a consequence of growing up with rage and her own inadequate feelings as a parent. When she feels out of control, a failure as a mother or trapped as a single parent, she is at risk for raging. After raging, she is overwhelmed with shame and feels even more inadequate.

The Child's Need For Boundaries

Sandy overcompensates for her raging behavior with her child by not setting appropriate limits, guidelines or measures of discipline for her child's acting-out behavior. She has difficulty establishing limits for her child's inappropriate behavior, and when she does set consequences, she rarely follows through with them. Children need to have limits established for them to feel safe. When parents do not set appropriate boundaries for children, children will push and act out, forcing parents to take responsibility and parent. Unfortunately for Sandy, since she does not know how to set limits as needed, her child, Lilly, continues to push until Sandy feels out of control. Sandy regains a feeling of control with raging behavior. Sandy's parenting skills are extreme, from being too lax to being abusive with raging behavior.

Sandy is also abusing Lilly by overempowering her, by allowing the child to have her way more often than not and by not following through with consequences for unacceptable behavior. Lilly will learn how to manipulate her mother to get what she wants by knowing just how to push the limits. She will also learn that after her mother has raged she is easier to manipulate, so she may even push her mother into raging behavior to achieve her goals.

Sandy overempowers her child by not being consistent in her disciplining and by giving in to her daughter's demands in order to keep peace. She disempowers Lilly by raging when feeling trapped and inadequate as a parent. Her daughter feels totally responsible for her mother's behavior, not knowing this behavior is about her mother's unresolved childhood issues.

Manipulation Versus Intimacy

Lilly will grow into an adult who believes it is necessary to manipulate others to get her needs taken care of. She will also feel initially responsible for others' feelings, eventually finding herself unconsciously creating barriers of rage, addiction or other dysfunctional distancing behaviors to protect herself. Intimacy will not be possible for Lilly because she does not have the skills necessary for healthy communication.

Not having had a father, she will seek out those men she perceives as fatherly on an unconscious basis. Having learned how to manipulate at a very early age, she will do what is necessary to get her way in relationships. Lilly may allow herself to be disempowered with sexual actions or abuse to get her needs taken care of, but she will not see these acts as disempowering. She may even feel in control, knowing she will get what she wants in the end.

Lilly may also develop a hard-shelled attitude towards the world, believing her needs and wants are the most important and that the only way to make it in life is to be cunning, demanding and at times even offensive to others. Lilly's attitudes about respect for the feelings of others may be limited, believing she has had to make her own way in the world and that it is not her responsibility if others are offended by her actions. Lilly may go through a number of relationships, staying only as long as the relationship takes care of her needs and wants. She will not understand that she is responsible for meeting her own needs in healthy ways but will become a user of people.

Individuals such as Lilly have a morbid fear of being vulnerable because being vulnerable to them means being weak. During childhood, vulnerability meant experiencing pain and the only way to avoid the pain was to distance self from the emotional, physical or sexual hurt with barriers of attitudes which said, "I can endure this, I'll show you . . . You can't hurt me because I won't let you . . . I'll play your game to get my way."

When parents are abuse survivors themselves, it is difficult for them to know how to parent in healthy ways, and they are at risk for doing to their children what was done to them, as in the case of Sandy and her daughter, Lilly.

DOUG'S STORY | Abused parents can also produce a child like Doug, who as an adult has a terrible time taking responsibility for himself. Doug's mother, Sarah, is a sexual abuse survivor. She has never told anyone about her abuse, except for her husband, Paul. Paul is also an abuse survivor who grew up in a family where his mother, a sexual abuse survivor, abused him physically and sexually. Paul hasn't any memory of being sexually abused, but does remember the physical beatings his mother inflicted upon him. Paul's father was an alcoholic who was always away from the home and at the bars. To this day Paul hates alcohol and does not drink. He carries with him a great deal of anger about the past, but does not talk about it, belieiving it is not worth it to "mull over old pain." Sarah tries to be the perfect mother for Doug, vowing she will never allow anybody to ever hurt him the way she was hurt. She screens all of his friends, and she and Paul rarely go out together for fear of leaving Doug with a baby sitter who could hurt him.

Paul worries about how Sarah smothers and overprotects Doug, but he doesn't say anything about it. He fears she is spoiling him by not allowing him to grow up or experience life.

The Special Child

Doug is 11 years old, and as an only child is often lonely. His parents tell him how special he is but at times he wishes they would treat him as his friends' parents treat their kids. Doug feels as though his parents expectations of him are overwhelming and believes being reminded of just how special he is puts more pressure on him. Doug's mother does everything for him and he suspects his mother loves him more than his father.

When much younger, all of the relatives focused their attention on Doug. He was the first grandchild in the family and everybody told him how cute and special he was. One evening while at a family gathering with his parents, grandparents, uncles and aunts, Doug's grandmother announced to everyone that Doug had something special to say. Doug was three at this time and loved the way all of the adults stopped what they were doing to listen to him. Whenever Grandma would announce he had something to say, all of the adults were expected to stop whatever they were doing, no matter how important it was, and pay attention to Doug. This went on throughout the years, and Doug grew accustomed to not only being the center of attention for his parents, but also for the extended family as a whole. He was the family star.

On the outside this appears to be a healthy family system, always available to meet the needs of the child — but, as we see, this excessive amount of attention over the years produces some problems. As Doug grew older, he was accustomed to all of the attention being on him by his family. As a result of this, he had difficulty playing with other children his own age. He didn't feel as though he fit, so he usually played with kids who were either younger or older. When playing with a same-aged peer group, the other children did not see Doug as being special — they saw him as just another kid their age. As a consequence, playing with same-aged children did not rotate around Doug's wants or needs. When playing with older children, he was treated differently as if he were unique. Plus bigger kids gave him his way more often than kids who were his age because he was younger. With younger children, Doug could control play because he was bigger than the younger kids. The younger kids looked up to him because he was bigger and, being bigger, he always had his way in play with them.

When with older or younger children, overempowered children feel in control because they are unique and by virtue of their uniqueness, are in a position of power. It is difficult for them to bond successfully with a peer group because they have an insatiable need for the self-centered attention they have received from their family of origin.

Remember, we learn about the real world by living in our family of origin. If in our family of origin we are overempowered with excessive attention and caretaking, we will have expectations of this in the real world. If we are raised always believing, "Somebody else will take care of it . . . I always come first to others . . . My wants are more important than the needs of others," we will continue these attitudes in adulthood.

Overempowerment Rebound

When Doug was 11, one of his aunts had a baby girl. Doug found, after 11 years of being told he was the most important member of the family, that with the birth of his cousin, he was no longer receiving all of the attention. It was as if overnight his role in the family changed. Doug hated his cousin as he watched all of his relatives, even his parents, talk about how special his cousin was.

Jealousy is a natural feeling young children have but for the overempowered child, the feeling can be overwhelming. Overempowered children have very fragile egos and since they have been overprotected, overindulged and overloaded with attention, they have not had to experience the frustration necessary for the development of healthy emotional growth. Frustration is necessary because it challenges children to explore their own potential and encourages the development of life skills. A child like Doug rarely develops those life skills necessary to survive change, challenge, disappointment or life adjustment because frustration was removed from his path during his younger years. As a result, when confronted with frustrating situations, he looks to others for resolution. He will probably manipulate others into taking responsibility for resolving his dilemmas. Doug will have difficulty meeting his needs in a healthy way and will resort to childhood manipulation to achieve his goals.

With the birth of his new cousin, he is no longer the center of his family's attention. Doug may have a tantrum, whine or manipulate to re-establish his role as star. To a degree, some of this behavior is normal when a child feels displaced by another as a consequence of a birth. If the child has been provided with experiences involving frustration, challenge, adjustment and growth, eventually the child will be able to accept the new addition to the family, learning that the attention must now be shared.

An overempowered child will not be able to overcome this hurdle and may begin acting out with controlling behavior, involving testing the limits with negative acting out. Or a child such as this may withdraw and search elsewhere for the attention needed to fulfill his or her insatiable desire for self-centered adoration.

Prioritizing Needs

Overempowered children have a constant tendency to control the mood of the family. In a healthy family situation, Mother's needs for Mother come before her relationship needs, as do Father's needs come first for Father before his wife's needs. The needs of the relationship are secondary to the needs of the individual because if parents individually do not take care of themselves, they cannot be there for one another in the relationship. Third are the needs, and sometimes wants, of the child. If the relationship is not stable, the needs of the child will not be taken care of. When there are unresolved difficulties in a relationship, much energy is directed towards those problems. When this happens, it is difficult to be totally available to the children.

As an active alcoholic, my life rotated around my drinking. I was obsessed with when I would drink, what I would drink, how much I would drink and whether or not I could make it to the bedroom before passing out. Michael, as an active workaholic before recovery, rotated his life around his work schedule. Work was more important than his physical or emotional well-being. We both went for marital therapy to attempt to resolve those issues causing us difficulty in our relationship.

Unfortunately we were seeing a therapist who had little understanding of addiction. When there is active addiction in a relationship, it is impossible to resolve relationship issues until the addictions are in remission. Not knowing this, we continued working on the relationship and found we were getting nowhere. In financial debt to this therapist, we discontinued treatment. Eventually, I had to take care of my own individual addictions, family of origin issues and dysfunctional lifeskills, as did Michael, before either of us could focus in on the relationship.

It is impossible to meet the needs of any relationship if individual needs have not been addressed. Secondly, if our relationship is unstable, it is necessary for both of us to address these issues in order for us to be emotionally available to our child.

Many people come into my office complaining about their children's behavior. The focus is on how Johnny's behaving at school, how Cindy's not sleeping or how Eric keeps hitting other kids in the neighborhood. The focus is on the children, when in reality there are either individual difficulties for one or both parents and/or relationship difficulties. Most parents are not aware that to place the child's wants before the parents' individual needs or relationship needs is overempowering and dis-empowering the child. At the same time, if parents do not take care of their individual needs, they are not modeling for their child healthy adult self-care.

An example of this would be the mother who buys her clothes at K-Mart so that she can afford to buy the designer jeans her daughter demands. Or the father who gives up his weekly men's therapy group to pay for his son's trip to Europe.

The mother in this example is modeling that she isn't as important as her child. Aside from disempowering her child with inappropriate modeling, she is overempowering her by giving in to her demands for very expensive clothing. This child will grow up believing all she has to do is demand her way in order to meet her goals. She will have expectations of others giving in to her demands, even at the expense of themselves. She will be confused and even shocked when people do not give in to her demands and may retaliate with inappropriate behavior. This behavior worked for her while growing up, so she will expect it to work in adulthood.

The father who gives up his men's therapy group to pay for his son's European trip is disempowering his son by modeling for him that his own emotional well-being is not as important as his son's wish for a trip to Europe. He is overempowering his son by placing more emotional and financial attention on his son's vacation plans than on his own emotional well-being.

Healthy Parental Modeling

When parents take care of themselves, they are modeling for their children adult self-care and self-respect. When we can care for ourselves and respect ourselves, this increases our feelings of self-worth and self-esteem. When parents do not take care of themselves in healthy ways, they are not teaching their children how to love themselves and grow into competent, healthy adults.

Many people balk when I tell them that their relationship comes before the wants and, sometimes, needs of their children. They tell me I am awful and don't understand, until I begin explaining to them how unavailable they already are to their children.

Relationships take work, and problems are typical in a relationship that is working. Adults need time and space to attend to the maintenance of their adult life, but unfortunately many adults fear dealing with their relationships and use the children as an excuse.

Examples of this would be the couple who never goes out without the child for fear of leaving the child with a sitter. ("I was sexually abused by a baby sitter and feared the same would happen to my child if left with a sitter.") This is a common response for abuse survivors.

I found several reliable sitters with excellent references and began leaving Aaron with them. Aaron, naturally not wanting me to leave, threw a fit the first time I left him. I felt like the worst parent in the world and I cried throughout the evening. Aaron, sensing my discomfort over leaving him, began crying louder when I would leave. I began checking on him, returning to the house 10 minutes after I left, only to discover he was fine, playing happily with the sitter. This crying behavior before leaving him with a sitter continued until he began realizing it wasn't going to work. This is not to say that every time a child cries, he or she is manipulating. What is important is to determine whether or not there is a real problem when children act out or whether it is an issue of control.

Parents need time to themselves to work and enjoy themselves and their relationship. In many situations, when children accompany parents, even to adult eateries, the children are brought along as distractions and buffers because the parents fear being alone together. The message the children receive is that their parents' lives rotate around them, when in reality what is happening is that the children are being emotionally used and abused. In situations such as this, children move into the world of adulthood and are at risk for emotional incest.

When adults do not take out time for their relationship, they are modeling for their children unhealthy relationship skills. By not taking care of their adult needs, they will have difficulty being available to their children in healthy ways.

The Co-dependent Mother

One woman came to my office with complaints about her out-of-control, hostile four-year-old. She stated she was in recovery for her co-dependency and divorced from her sexually addicted husband. I asked her if she went to 12-Step meetings and she said no because she could not leave her child alone. I asked her if she ever traveled for vacation or business and she said no because she could not leave her child. I asked her if she dated at all and she said rarely because she feared leaving her child. I told her she was co-dependent on her child, placing all of her child's needs before her own. I also shared with her that by not having a life of her own, she was overempowering her child by rotating her life around him. With this, she smiled sadly and agreed. I then told her she was also disempowering her child by expecting her child to fulfill all of her emotional needs so that she would not have to risk exploring life. With this she became angry with me and I knew we were on the right track.

Michael and I have a date night each week and we also take vacation time away together without Aaron. This allows us time to reconnect with one another as an adult couple. We may fight and work on resolving our relationship problems or play and enjoy each other's company. When the needs of the relationship are satisfied, we are both free to give Aaron the parental attention he needs without emotional interference from our problems.

For the single parent, time away from the children is also necessary. My mother had very little balance in her life. When she and my father divorced, she covered her pain with alcohol. She worked two jobs and would tell my sisters and me that this time away at work was necessary to make ends meet and that I, as the older sister, was in charge.

Periodically she would become overwhelmed with the responsibilities of being a single parent and abandon us with excessive dating and nights out. Feeling shame about abandoning us with such behavior, she would return to her role as the overly responsible single parent.

My mother did not know how to meet her adult needs in healthy ways and as a result lived in a world of extremes. Both of these worlds were abusive to me, my sisters and to her. When she was working excessively, I was overempowered as mother's little helper and when she abandoned us, I felt disempowered, alone, scared and confused about how to parent my sisters. My mother did not know how to meet her adult needs in healthy ways and she did not have those life skills necessary for problem resolution. So she was unavailable emotionally, and sometimes physically, as a parent.

ERIC'S STORY Many children are also overempowered with responsibility for a parent. Eric is very concerned about his wife's health as she has been experiencing heart problems for several years. He relies heavily on his two sons, Peter and Mark, for emotional support.

Peter and Mark both phone home several times a week to talk with their parents. Peter, the older of the two, especially feels responsible for brightening his mother's day. When he calls, his father thanks him profusely for making her feel better. In response to their phone calls, Eric sends his sons gifts of money. Both young men know that if they talk to their mother and "brighten her day," they will receive checks in the mail. They dread making the phone calls but feel it is their duty.

Eric has too much false pride to ask for help in caring for his wife and insists that this is a family matter. Peter wishes his father would seek out professional help for himself and his mother. He tires of being his father's father and his mother's entertainer. His younger brother, Mark, complains to him about not being allowed to have a life of his own with his parents' constant demands of his attention.

One week Mark was sick with the flu and did not call home. His father tried to call several times but Mark wanted only to sleep and recover from his illness, so he did not answer the phone. When he recovered from the flu he made his usual call home. His father was very upset with him and asked why he had not called. When Mark told his father he had been sick with the flu, his father said, "You should have called to let us know what was going on! Think about my feelings for once!"

Mark, angry with his father, complained to Peter, "That's the problem. We *always* have to think about them. I couldn't even be sick in peace."

Eric does not have the lifeskills necessary for dealing with his sick wife. He has overempowered his two sons with the responsibility of her well-being. Both Peter and Mark feel responsible, not only for their mother's health but also for their father's emotional well-being. They are given money for being loyal sons but the emotional price paid in return is almost overwhelming.

This family is very enmeshed and the boundaries are almost nonexistent. These young men will not be able to have successful intimate relationships as long as they are bound into their parents financially and are responsible for their parents' emotional well-being. Although they will do well at taking care of others, they will have difficulty taking care of themselves emotionally in healthy ways.

The Caretakers

Individuals such as this usually go into the helping professions where they have incredible power over the destinies of others, but are at a loss in repairing their own damaged lives.

As nurses, doctors, therapists, teachers, religious leaders and others in the helping professions, they may have difficulty asking for help for themselves, but are more than willing to offer help to others. Individuals such as these unknowingly can cause damage and confusion to those they attempt to help because of their own unresolved family of origin issues. The intoxicating power which can come as a result of helping others in need can produce an almost invincible godlike sense to the overempowered helping professional, making it difficult to see any defects of character and unresolved problems.

Individuals in the helping profession must have their own house in order, addictions in remission, family of origin issues addressed and have healthy boundaries established before offering aid to another. The helping profession is full of overempowered individuals who set themselves up to be the Higher Power for those they are supposed to be serving. Helping professionals are naturally in a position of power because of the knowledge they possess about their field. This power can easily be abused with the person in need suffering the consequences.

JOYCE'S STORY | Joyce was a graduate student in psychology at a local university. Through her studies she began to see she had a great deal of unresolved childhood issues because of her parents' alcoholism. She began seeing a therapist who agreed it would be necessary for her to address these issues and her therapy began on a weekly basis.

She had heard about Adult Children of Alcoholics meetings and asked her therapist about this. Her therapist discouraged her participation in these 12-Step groups, stating they were nonprofessional and that she could gain the information and support she needed for such issues in therapy. As her therapy continued, Joyce did begin feeling better and would periodically even call her therapist at home in times of trouble. Her therapist had given her a home phone number and had encouraged her to use it when necessary.

During one of their therapy sessions she was asked if she would take over the three therapy groups her therapist ran while she was at a conference. Joyce felt strange about this but agreed to do so, believing her therapist must know what was she was doing by asking. Joyce felt uncomfortable being a patient and her therapist's replacement at the same time, but decided this would aid her in her graduate psychology studies. All went well with the groups but Joyce was beginning to feel confused about her relationship with her therapist. At one point her therapist told Joyce to divorce her husband or else she would never be able to grow individually. When her therapist suggested this, Joyce felt scared and uneasy, but began exploring the possibility of a separation.

Joyce also saw her therapist socially, as her therapist would have parties and invite her to such gatherings. At one party Joyce noticed that her therapist had quite a bit to drink. Under the influence of margaritas, she began talking about her relationship with her parents. Joyce began to see that her therapist had not resolved her own feelings about her unresolved childhood issues. At their next therapy session she confronted her therapist with this. Her therapist said it was none of her business and that if she wasn't satisfied with the way things were, she could look elsewhere for therapy.

The Helping Professional's Boundary Abuses

I have seen many individuals who have an honest desire for help be abused by helping professionals who are over-empowered and unresolved about their own family of origin business. I have seen boundaries violated and abused as a result of the helping professional's own dysfunctional boundaries with comments such as:

1. I am the doctor, therapist, teacher, nurse, etc., so I know what you need or what is best for you.
2. You don't really feel that way.
3. You have an overactive imagination.
4. Support groups don't work.
5. We don't need to talk about that.
6. You don't know what you are talking about.
7. If you want to work with me, we will do it my way.
8. I went to school to study this so you need to trust me.

These are comments which state, "I'm in authority, don't question my power, ideas, methods, motives or values." Helping professionals are human and fallible, but if they

set themselves up to be bigger than life and unquestion-
able, most likely they are overempowered and addicted to
the power of controlling others.

If I cannot question the actions of an authority figure
or helping professional without defensive rebuttal from
them as a consequence, I am probably dealing with a non-
recovering overempowered individual who has unresolved
family of origin issues.

In Joyce's case, her therapist did not want her to attend
12-Step support groups. Helping professionals who dis-
courage such self-help groups are usually fearful of losing
control over their clientele and have a need to be the only
source of help and information to them. Support groups
for such professionals pose a threat and so are discounted.

Also untreated helping professionals tend to force their
dysfunctional beliefs on those in their care. For example,
to tell a client to separate or divorce from a mate is a
boundary violation because the professional is assuming
too much power in the client's life. Helping professions
should provide options, not controlling direction. Many
helping professionals abuse their clients by not having
clear boundaries for themselves.

In Joyce's case her best interests were not being served
when she was asked to run therapy groups in her therapist's absence. Her therapist's needs were being taken care
of, but it was confusing Joyce's role in therapy as a patient.

Also when a helping professional discounts a client by
saying, "You really shouldn't feel that way" or "I don't
want to hear that; we either do it my way or you can go
elsewhere," the person in need is being shamed and discounted. When a helping professional is not willing to be
confronted or listen to an opposing point of view, this is
usually an indication that he or she fears losing control of
the situation. A healthy professional will listen to opposing views and discuss such ideas with the client.

Several years ago I was having stomach problems. The
physician I was seeing had difficulty listening to my ideas
about the origins of my illness. He would not even return
my phone calls or communicate the information I needed

to understand my predicament. Being a recovering prescription drug addict, I was not able to take pain medication and had to just endure the physical pain and wait. After quite some time had passed, I was told, "You either do as I say or go elsewhere." I felt hurt, shamed and without the right to input into my situation. Eventually I did find a physician who was very willing to listen to my concerns. Upon changing physicians and finally getting the help I needed, as a result of his willingness to listen, my illness quickly cleared up. Although I do not have a medical degree, I did have some information which was useful in diagnosing my situation effectively.

Distancing

If we are to feel a part of our recovery from our dysfunctional boundaries, we must develop those tools necessary for effectively communicating with others. If we have been overempowered in our youth, we may need to learn how to give up some of the control we feel we so desperately need. We must examine why it was not safe to experience openness in our families of origin. Otherwise, we will repeat those same behaviors of distancing when confronted with intimacy or vulnerability. For those of us who have been overempowered, to not be in control will feel frightening. We initially will not know how to behave. We will fear being hurt and may even begin experiencing pain as a consequence of opening up and sharing ourselves with others.

Some of us will feel useless at not being in control and will find ourselves having to keep quiet as we watch others do things differently than we would have done. Patience, tolerance and humility will be those characteristics we will slowly and painfully develop. We also will have to learn how to listen and really hear what others around us are saying. Initially this will be scary because some of us will fear what we hear. It also will be important for us to learn how to ask for support and help. Most overempowered individuals have difficulty with this. Fears of rejection and of looking incompetent well up inside us.

Our overempowerment separates us from our true selves, humanity and our spirituality. If we put barriers around ourselves, they block out chances for intimacy and vulnerability, leaving us trapped and alone with our own fears, old hurts and new pains. While growing up we created an emotional safety for ourselves with our barriers and survived our dysfunctional families with the intoxicating feelings of being overempowered. But in adulthood, our barriers have become prison walls. The need for power is addictive but it separates us from being a part of the life experience. If you are one of those who are still hiding from the world behind the false sense of confidence of the overempowered child, it is my hope that you will break free to join the world of risk, vulnerability, intimacy and fallibility — for this is truly living.

Anything To Avoid Pain | 8

Distancing Behaviors

One response to growing up in a crazy-making, addicted, abusive family is to distance ourselves from others. "If I don't get too close, I won't get hurt." People who use distancing behaviors, such as raging, emotional withdrawal, physical isolation, criticism and aloofness, distraction with activities, withdrawal into excessive fantasy or daydreaming, do so when feeling intimacy involving self-disclosure and honesty is wanted by another in a relationship.

When I was very active in my addictions, I lived in two worlds. As I mentioned earlier, I was a card-carrying member of victims anonymous. After much abuse, misery and pain as a result of this role, I would isolate and withdraw from humankind, vowing never to trust again. I would push those closest to me away with raging behavior, criticism and hostility. Although on the outside I appeared to be one tough old broad, deep within my soul I was dying for intimacy. I would push away what I so desperately craved, fearing abandonment, rejection, abuse or having my reality discounted. During these times, I feared trusting anyone at all. My barriers defending me against the possibility of pain also included my addictions. Because they blunted my aloneness during such times, they provided me with a false haven of safety.

When we do not know how to protect ourselves in healthy ways, we use those childhood survival skills most familiar to us, especially during times of stress or danger. Many of us learned how to protect ourselves at the expense of others. The attitude is "I'll hurt you before you hurt me . . . Since you abused me, I'm going to get you back." Put more bluntly, "An eye for an eye and a tooth for a tooth."

Some helping professions refer to this frame of mind as offender behavior.

Unfortunately when most of us think of offender behavior, we think only of murderers, rapists, robbers or others committing felony crimes. We never think that our own survival skills from childhood may be infiltrated with a bit of offender behavior.

As a matter of fact, I always thought of myself as *just* a victim, ignoring those characteristics of mine which, based on my own need for survival in childhood, were offensive in the here and now to others. It was necessary to break through my own denial to examine my offensive behaviors rooted in my own unfinished family of origin business. So many of us walk around feeling victimized by others, unaware that possibly we also may be hurting those around us with some of our own behaviors. It was difficult for me to embrace this ominous part of myself. I had to admit I felt comfortable being in the role of perpetual victim because then I always had somebody else to blame. But to be the one who is offending others?

When I initially embraced this part of myself, I felt overwhelmed with shame. The word *offender* made me cringe with shame and I felt like the lowest person on the face of the earth. After all of my complaining about being offended by others, I discovered I, too, was capable of the same behavior. Since I found the word offender so shaming, I decided I felt more comfortable referring to that part of myself as a *boundary violator.*

My boundary violator eventually allowed herself to be known to me, and what I discovered was that in times of fear she could be a real intruder. Some of her boundary violating behavior was purposeful and with intent, while other behavior was a product of lack of awareness.

Intentional Boundaries Violation

An example of intentional boundary violation on my part would be the time I poured a full glass of milk on Michael's head. In early recovery I experienced an overwhelming co-dependent fear that Michael would never learn how to express his feelings. One evening I was trying to work Michael's recovery program for him by explaining the importance of expressing feelings. He sat, looking void of any emotion. In response I angrily dumped an entire 16-ounce glass of cold milk on his head! My boundary violator had made her presence known. Needless to say, Michael felt shocked, angry and hurt upon realizing I would go to such abusive lengths to get a reaction out of him. I felt shame when I saw just what I had done.

Healthy Shame

It is important for us to experience shame about those violating behaviors of ours which cause others pain, shame, fear or anger. Our shame in these situations teaches us about those behaviors which are inappropriate and unacceptable. Unfortunately many repeated criminal acts or repeated violations are done by individuals who are out of touch with their own sense of healthy shame. For those of us who continue to behave shamelessly over and over again, it is important for our healing to reconnect with our healthy shame.

Healthy shame gives us a sense of our humanness, connectedness with our environment, and it gives us a sense of humility. It forces us to recognize that the lives of others or the world in general does not rotate around our needs and wants. Our healthy shame teaches us how to live in harmony with others. When we feel our shame about our own inappropriate behavior, we are forced to examine our activities and our "dark side." We all have a dark side and each of us at one time or another expresses it in some violating way.

In the example I have given of my dark side, my boundary violator really was out of line. Pouring milk on Michael was an inappropriate method of self-expression. When we find ourselves violating the boundaries of others with intent, it is necessary for us to examine our motives.

Nonintentional Boundary Violation

An example of boundary violation not done with intent would be the following:

In some family systems it is difficult to tell whose is whose because the boundaries are so dysfunctional or nonexistent. Growing up in my family, my sisters and I never respected one another's privacy and would constantly *borrow* from each other without asking. It seemed normal to take without asking until I married Michael.

One evening early in our relationship we were out for dinner at a seafood restaurant. The shrimp we were eating were excellent and I quickly devoured mine, garlic sauce and all. Michael still had some shrimp on his plate and I reached over with my fork and took one. He looked shocked!

"What is wrong with you?" I asked.

"I can't believe you just took one of my shrimp without asking!"

So here we were, sitting in this fancy eatery, arguing over a shrimp. Michael was in the right as I had violated his boundary by taking without asking. But since this was "normal behavior," according to my family of origin upbringing, I was totally unaware that I was behaving inappropriately.

Many of us violate others knowingly out of fear but, more so than not, our boundary violations are a result of not knowing any better.

I was visiting some friends for dinner. Being a recovering alcoholic, I did not want any of the champagne that was being served, so I asked the host if anything nonalcoholic was available. Having developed some boundaries, I had learned it was important to ask before rummaging through the hostess' cupboards and refrigerator. She told me there was some freshly squeezed orange juice in the refrigerator and encouraged me to help myself. I found a glass and the juice and served myself. Before I could return the juice to its place in the refrigerator, another guest came along, picked up my glass of juice and poured half of it into her own glass without even asking. When they say, "What goes around comes around," they're right. I felt so violated and was absolutely speechless. Having developed some healthy boundaries, taking without asking was now no longer acceptable behavior in my recovering scheme of the world. But for this other guest, who appeared to be very comfortable with draining half of my glass of juice with a smile, this was "normal" for her.

Boundary Violations

It is important for us to examine our own boundary violating behavior in order to re-evaluate how we interact with those around us. Some examples of boundary violations would be as follows:

1. Taking or "borrowing" the property or possessions of others without their permission.

For years I would take Michael's shirts and wear them without asking first. He would look in his closet for one of his shirts and discover I had used it without his permission. He would feel angry while looking at the wrinkled perfume-doused shirt he had planned to wear for that day. I had violated his boundaries by not asking if it was all right with him if I wore one of his shirts. To take something from somebody else without their permission, be that materially, financially or emotionally, is a boundary violation.

Periodically I receive phone calls from friends, family and associates who are in need of emotional support. When talking with them, it is my responsibility to set limits as to how much time I am willing to offer. If I only have one hour or five minutes to talk, it is my responsibility to share this limit with whomever I am in conversation with. If, after I have shared this boundary, I find it is not respected, I immediately know I am dealing with a boundary violator. When somebody sets an emotional boundary with us, it is important for us to respect that. Not to respect this request sets us up to be "takers" as opposed to "sharers." It is important to ask:

- "May I borrow this?"
- "Do you mind if I take this?"
- "Would it be all right with you if I use this?"
- "Do you have a moment to listen?"
- "How much time can you spare?"
- "Are you busy? If not, do you mind if I talk with you about this matter for a while?"
- "Can I come over and chat?"

It is important to ask. When we ask, we are telling the other person, "I have a need I must have assistance with, but I respect you enough to ask before assuming you are willing to help me out."

2. Touching, hugging or kissing another without asking permission.

How many of us have touched, hugged or kissed another without thinking about how the receiver of our touch may feel about the interchange? A number of us assume that if we want to hug someone, they automatically must also want to hug us back. In some cases this assumption is true, but in many it is not. Often I have been approached for a hug or a kiss and have not been in a receptive mood for such physical contact. When I have said to such people, "Please don't hug, kiss or touch me as I am in need of space," they appear shocked and in some cases hurt with my request to take care of myself. Just because we are wanting intimate physical contact does not necessarily mean those we want to reach out to and touch are receptive. It is always important to ask before touching, otherwise we might be at risk for violating the boundaries of another.

With sexual intimacy, a number of us also assume that when we feel like being sexual, automatically our sex partner feels the same way. Not necessarily! It is important for us to check this out by asking. So many of us assume others can read our minds and that in turn, we can predict the needs of others before asking. In reality we may be *way off base!* Even if our intuitions about another's needs or wants are correct, we will be expressing our respect for their rights as individuals and offering them the gift of choice if we ask first.

- "Can I give you a hug?"
- "Would you mind if I touch you?"
- "Is it all right if I kiss you?"

These are statements which say, "I'm respecting your boundaries by asking first."

3. Looking in another's purse, pocketbook, briefcase, journal, etc., without permission of the owner.

For many years in our relationship Michael thought it was his job to balance my checkbook. He would find my checkbook in my purse, take it out and balance it. There was much controversy over his need to get my checkbook out of my purse because I felt violated and intruded upon when he did so. I would gripe and grumble under my breath, expecting him to stop this behavior without my being more direct with my feelings. One day this small issue became a huge problem and there was a showdown at the Brandon house.

I had gone grocery shopping one afternoon at the local food market. This shopping expedition was "the big one," involving shopping for all household essentials and food products necessary for the month. After spending quite some time collecting my purchases, it was necessary for me to stand in a 25-minute checkout line with others who had just done their "big shopping," too. As I was being checked out I noticed my checkbook was missing. Fearful I had lost it, I remembered Michael's past behavior of rummaging through my purse in search of my checkbook for balancing. Angry as a hornet disturbed from the nest, I raced home, flashed Michael a very hostile look, grabbed my checkbook, and returned to stand in another 25-minute line to pay for my groceries.

After that incident, Michael and I sat down and set boundaries with my purse and checkbook, and his wallet and briefcase. Today we know it is important to ask if we are in need of looking at or using another's property. Even though Michael thought he was doing me a favor by balancing my checkbook, he was still violating my boundaries. Questions such as. . .

- "Do you mind if I check your wallet for the credit card?"
- "Can I look in your purse for a hairbrush?"
- "May I get some paper out of your briefcase?"
- "How do you feel about sharing your journal with me?"

. . . offer choices and let another know you are in need, but do not wish to violate their boundaries with intrusive behavior.

4. *Not honoring another's request for emotional or physical space, forcing self emotionally or physically on another.*

"I need some privacy. Please leave me alone . . . I'd like some time to myself . . . I don't want to talk about it now . . . I don't feel sexual right now . . . Please sleep upstairs; I need some space from you for a while" are all requests for boundaries of space, requiring emotional and, in some cases, physical separation from others. We are all in need of emotional and physical solitude at different points in our lives. Sometimes when someone close to us asks for space or privacy, our own fears of being abandoned surface and we become overwhelmed with insecurity. We may retaliate by smothering the individual requesting solitude, alienating them from us even more.

Sometimes when Michael asks for space, my own abandonment feelings kick in and my co-dependency says, "He is rejecting you and leaving you forever." My immediate response is to try to find out why he needs space from *me!* Sometimes his need for alone time is related to me, but more often than not, he is just in need of some quiet time for himself to sort out his thoughts.

In relationships of all kinds people periodically need space, either from the relationship itself or in order to gain clarity within their own lives. It is important for us to respect those wishes and allow others to take care of themselves. It also may be important for us to examine our own abandonment fears when confronted with how another's need for space impacts us. Our own overwhelming fears of abandonment are most likely tied to our abandonment issues in early childhood.

5. Not returning personal possessions to their owners after having been allowed their usage with the promise of their return to their owner.

Marsha loaned Jenny several household items as Jenny was moving into her first apartment. Marsha loaned Jenny a set of dishes, a vacuum cleaner and a dinette set with the understanding that these items would be returned within two months. Jenny assured her friend that within two months she would have purchased those items to replace the loaned household goods Marsha had allowed her to use. Six months later Jenny still had not purchased her own household goods and still was using Marsha's. Marsha was resentful because she needed her dishes and dinette set back for a party she was giving for her daughter's birthday. Each time she asked Jenny for her things back, Jenny would assure her they would be returned within a week. Eventually Marsha found it necessary to be very direct with her angry feelings towards Jenny about breaking their agreement to have the articles returned in two months. Needless to say, the friendship came to an end.

When others loan their possessions to us, it is our responsibility to return them at the agreed time, and if not then, as soon as possible. It is also our job to take care of their possessions and to replace the borrowed article if we lose or damage it. Not to respect a return agreement at the appointed time is a boundary violation. This behavior sets us up to appear as "takers" who do not respect the property of our friends or regard the needs of others as important. By returning borrowed property as promptly as possible, we are letting the lender know how much we value them and how grateful we are to them for helping us out in a time of need.

6. Interrupting another who is speaking by talking over them, without excusing self and asking for permission to interject into the conversation.

In my family of origin people yelled. They usually yelled in order to be heard. My sister, who works very diligently on herself, and I periodically find ourselves talking over one another in order to be heard, repeating our own family of origin dynamic, each fearful the other isn't listening. Then we both will remember we are in recovery and allow equal time for each to speak.

Many of us have been around someone who ends our sentences for us or who interrupts us while we are talking. The feelings which follow such interruptions can range from anger, feelings of rejection, feeling discounted, shame, feeling abused, hurt and so on. Some of us clam up in response to such behavior, while others of us retaliate by becoming boundary violators. Neither behavior is productive, but it is acceptable to state one's feelings about such a violation. Others of us, as a consequence of our co-dependency or need to caretake, will not only complete someone else's sentences, talk above a conversation to be heard or interrupt others, but also will speak for another. In our minds, we usually see ourselves as helping another out when in reality, we may be violating their boundaries. We discount the existence of our friends and family when we talk over them or speak for them. We also discount their intelligence, values and opinions when we complete friends' sentences or interrupt a conversation abruptly. Statements such as . . .

- "I would like to say something about that issue."
- "I have something to share with regards to this matter."
- "When you are through talking, I would like to talk."
- "Excuse me, are you finished sharing? I need some time to express my point of view."

. . . are just a few of the ways we can be heard by others without violating boundaries. Another way to be heard in relationships is to agree before the conversation starts just how long each will share.

For example, if my sister and I are going to have a conversation and we are both in need of sharing time, we will agree beforehand that each of us will share without interruption from the other, unless asked, for ten minutes. In this way the boundary is agreed upon beforehand, with both parties understanding there are concrete limits. Healthy relationships are built on listening to one another. Some of us spend too much time listening while others rarely listen at all. All of us need to be heard in our relationships and we must also be listeners. Recovery is about achieving a balance between listening and sharing and learning not to always give or always take, but to share.

7. Shaming others.

How often have we been in conversations when someone says something to us that feels awful, icky, hurtful, condemning or shaming? Shaming another with statements such as . . .

- "You don't really mean what you say."
- "You can't actually feel that way."
- "You're just imagining what you saw, felt or heard."
- "You aren't supposed to say that."
- "You could/should/ought to have known better."

. . . are very shaming and belittling statements. Most individuals from dysfunctional families do not know how to express anger or disagreement in healthy ways. Using shaming statements is an unhealthy expression of anger or disagreement. Sometimes shaming statements are used to gain control over a situation or to promote a better, smarter, I-know-more-than-you attitude in relationships when we feel insecure, intimidated or frightened. Many of us came from families where shaming statements were dealt out on a regular basis, and for us today, these comments seem normal, even harmless.

Pauline and Calvin had been dating for several months and both had been enjoying the relationship. Periodically Calvin teases Pauline about her shoe size. Pauline becomes upset with Calvin and tells him he is hurting her feelings. He responds by telling her she shouldn't get so upset, that she is behaving like a big whining baby. Pauline feels hurt when Calvin calls her a baby. Her foot size had always been the butt of many a family joke and it hurts her to hear teasing again. She also was told in her family of origin, "Big girls don't cry," and sent to her room when she expressed sadness. Eventually, Pauline realizes that Calvin is treating her the same way her family did with regard to her foot size.

This scenario appears initially harmless but in reality it involves pain and shame for Pauline and confusion for Calvin.

In Calvin's family, everybody picked on one another as if it were normal family fun. Upon talking with his men friends in his Co-dependents Anonymous group, Calvin realizes his teasing of Pauline was shaming and inappropriate and that in his family of origin he, too, was shamed in the name of fun. As Pauline and Calvin talk, they both realize they are each acting out their unfinished family of origin business within the relationship. Pauline agrees to learn how to protect herself from offensive remarks directed her way while Calvin decides he needs to pay more attention to his comments to others and to watch for shaming remarks.

8. Shaming others by telling them they are stupid, crazy or ridiculous for having their opinions, ideas or thoughts. Threatening another for having an opinion.

"Alice, I'm going to send you to the moon if you say another word" was a bona fide attitude in the late 1950s made famous by Jackie Gleason. Threatening others for expressing their feelings as some parents do to children with statements like, "If you're going to cry, I'll really give you something to cry about," sets the stage for dishonesty as a result of fear in adult years. It is emotionally abusive to threaten to hit, kick or abuse another to keep that other from expressing his or her feelings.

A man wanted to give me a hug after a meeting one afternoon and came towards me with open arms. I felt uncomfortable in hugging him and said "No, thank you, I'm not in a place to be hugged." He responded with, "I should hit you," and angrily walked off. I felt scared, violated and intimidated. To tell a person they are stupid or crazy for having their opinions or ideas is emotionally abusive and it discounts their intellect and creativity. It also discounts one's uniqueness. To shame another because of race, creed, religion or social status is also a boundary violation and shows a lack of appreciation for individual differences. Comments like . . .

- "God gave homosexuals AIDS as a punishment."
- "All Jews are money hungry."
- "Mexicans are just wetbacks."
- "They are just white trash."
- "Those Vietnamese will steal you blind."
- "All women are stupid airheads."
- "Men are after only one thing."

. . . are just a few of the emotionally abusive statements which float around in our society. It is important for us to look at our own values, prejudices and family of origin upbringing to determine if any of our comments violate the boundaries of others.

9. Disclosing confidences.

Relationships are built on trust, and nothing can destroy a relationship quicker than disclosing confidences. I have had many clients say to me, "I'm scared to tell you anything. Everytime I tell somebody in my family something in private, the whole family knows." I assure them they can sue me if any of the issues we discuss hits the streets, with the exception of suicidal acting out, injury to a child or the contemplation of violent acts against another person. Upon realizing they are safe, they can begin to share.

When we are asked to keep something private and agree to it, we are establishing a verbal contract with the person who has shared with us. Many of us find ourselves saying, "Let me tell you about him, but don't say I told you because I promised him I'd keep quiet . . . I just have to tell you what she said, but don't say I said anything." When someone shares confidential information, they are trusting us to be responsible with that information. If we break that confidence, we are breaking trust and violating boundaries. Periodically, someone will share something that feels scary or of concern and we will feel a need to talk with another about it. If we feel we cannot keep such confidences, we need to be up front about this, letting the person who is sharing the confidence know, "I can't keep this confidence."

We need to use common sense when agreeing to keeping confidences. There is a difference between keeping quiet about frustrations with a family of origin, a fight with a spouse, anger towards a friend and a father sexually abusing a child, a mother overdosing on Valium, or a man planning to shoot and kill his next-door neighbor. Learning how to have healthy friendships involves learning how to have healthy boundaries. One is dependent upon the other. Re-examining our families of origin gives us the information we need to determine what it is about ourselves that must be changed in order to ensure healthy friendships.

10. Splitting or triangulation.

It is a major boundary violation to give to one party information about another with expectations of the first party passing this information on to the second. This happens so often between people who have difficulty being direct with one another about their feelings.

Stanley is angry with Mark but is afraid of confronting him. Both Mark and Stanley have a friend in common named Jason. Periodically Stanley calls Jason to complain about Mark, knowing Jason will pass this information on to Mark. When Mark calls Jason he, too, questions Jason about Stanley with the knowledge that what he says will be relayed back to Stanley. Jason doesn't want to lose his friendships with either of the men and feels trapped and abused as he did when his parents would send messages through him to one another. Both of Jason's friends are violating their friendship with him. Jason needs to pull out of the triangle, and Stanley and Mark need to be direct with one another. Our society as a whole has great difficulty in expressing feelings towards one another. We violate the boundaries of others as a consequence of this.

Our Personal Boundaries Violator

For generations we have been encouraged to say only "nice things," not to rock the boat, that pretty is as pretty does and "If you can't do anything right, don't do it at all . . . Do it until you get it perfect . . . A good job is worth doing right," and so on. These beliefs and values have set us up to fear our own imperfection and, as a result, we cover up our insecurities with boundary violating behavior. Most of us violate the boundaries of others without realizing it, believing our behavior is normal because this is what we learned growing up. We rarely see ourselves as boundary violators because compared with rapists, robbers and murderers we say, "I'm not like that." We feel more comfortable with the role of victim, not realizing there have been times when we, too, have victimized others.

I will never be perfect, and I will most likely periodically violate the boundaries of others in the future. By examining my own family of origin behavior, I have been able to define my personal boundary violator and can now keep a better eye on her. When she does get out of line, I can allow her the shame she needs to learn from her mistakes, to make amends and to grow emotionally from her experience. I have finally made friends with her and discovered she is a great teacher who keeps me humble as we both continue to experience living.

Self-Analysis Questionnaire
For Insight And Recovery | 9

For those of us who come from dysfunctional families, the concept of boundaries, let alone healthy boundaries, is probably totally incomprehensible to us. As mentioned at the beginning of this book, I had been abstaining from addictive acting-out behavior for several years before even hearing the word boundary. I found I was not only being victimized by others while in recovery, but also was unknowingly violating the boundaries of friends, family and peers myself. In order to determine exactly what my concept of a boundary was, I had to re-examine my childhood years and the development of my boundaries in my family of origin. What I discovered was frightening. I didn't know what a healthy boundary was. My family system had fluctuated throughout my youth, from chaotic enmeshment to controlling rigidity, and before I could begin to develop healthy boundaries, I discovered I was going to have to take an in-depth look at what I had to work with.

In order for us to determine what it is we have to work with, we need to ask ourselves some simple questions.

The first several questions we will need to ask focus in on our family of origin's perceptions of privacy. Was our family lacking in providing privacy for each individual family member or were our family members so guarded and secretive that today we feel uncomfortable opening up and sharing with others in any way, shape or form? Most of us will find our families at times were chaotic in some respects, while in other situations they were extremely guarded and secretive. As we explore our youths, we will be able to see parallels in behavior with our adult life.

Privacy

Exploring Your Family Of Origin

1. Do you feel you were allowed privacy in your family of origin? _____ Describe how _____
   _____

2. Were you allowed privacy in your room or did family members walk in and out freely? _____ If you did not have privacy in your room, how did that feel? _____
   _____

3. If your parents rarely came into your room, did you feel they just weren't interested? _____

4. Did people knock before coming into your room? ____ If not, how did you feel about it? _____
   _____

5. Did you feel safe in your room? _____ Why? _____
   _____

6. Did you feel safe undressing in your room or were you afraid someone would walk in unannounced while you were changing clothes? _____ If people walked in unannounced, how did you feel? _____
   _____

7. Were you allowed to have a lock on your door? __

8. If you didn't have a lock on your door, did you ever wish for one? _____ Why? _____

_____

9. When you were younger did you suffer from any of the following?

_____ Night terrors

_____ Fear of snakes in your room

_____ Fear of spiders in your room

_____ Difficulty sleeping in your bed

_____ Wetting the bed past toddler years

_____ Fear of vampires, robbers or monsters getting you in your room

_____ Fear of the dark

_____ Fear of getting out of the bed in the middle of the night to go to the bathroom

_____ A need to cover your head with blankets or pillows for protection

_____ Wearing extra clothing for protection.

The above are symptoms of childhood sexual abuse. If you answered yes to several of the above, you may have some undealt-with, repressed abuse issues in need of exploration. Abuse of any kind damages our boundaries.

10. Did you ever hear your parents quarrel late in the night when you were in bed? _____ If so, how did you feel about it then? _____

_____

How do you feel about it now? _____

_____

11. Did either of your parents ever come into your room to complain about the other parent or to dis-

cuss problems they were experiencing in their lives with you? _____ If so, how did you feel about that? _____

_____

If it made you feel uncomfortable, explain why ___

_____

If it made you feel special, explain how _____

_____

If your parents never shared themselves with you, did you feel isolated, alone, abandoned, rejected or left out? _____
If not, how else did you feel? _____

_____

12. Close your eyes and imagine the room or rooms you grew up in. Did you share the room with anybody else? _____ If so, did you enjoy that experience? _____ If you enjoyed the experience, describe how it was enjoyable _____
If you didn't enjoy the experience, describe why ___

_____

Your Space

If you shared a room, did you have your own space? _____ If not, what was that like?_____

_____

If you did have your own space, how did you differentiate your space from that of the person you shared the room with?_____

_____

13. Did you have your own closet and drawer space? _____ Did you have to share your clothes with a sibling? _____ If so, how do you feel about that?

_____

_____

Did people in your family borrow things of yours without asking? _____ If so, how do you feel about that? _____

_____

14. If people were very rigid in your family about using each other's property, how do you feel about that?

_____

Do you wish they would have shared more often with one another? _____

15. Do you share a room with somebody now? _____
If so, do you have your own closet space and drawer space? _____ If not, describe your situation _____

_____

Does your spouse, lover or roommate respect your private space and ask before entering your closet or drawer space? _____ If not, how does it feel? ____

_____

Do you ever enter your spouse's, lover's or room-mate's closet space or drawers without permission? _____ How do they react? _____

_____

16. Do you feel you can leave your personal private belongings out in your room and still have your privacy respected? _____ If not, how do you feel about that? _____

_____

If you leave your wallet, purse, journal or briefcase out in the open, do you trust your privacy will be respected? _____

17. Do you ever look through other family members' closets, drawers, wallets, briefcases, purses, etc.? _____ If so, why? _____

_____

How do you feel about your "why" answer? _____

_____

Do other family members ever refer to you as a snoop, busybody or become angry upon learning you have been in their personal belongings? _____ If so, how do you feel about their responses? _____

_____

Your Bed

18. In childhood did you have your own bed to sleep in? _____ If not, who did you share a bed with?
_____

All children need their own sleeping space and their own bed. It is abusive not to provide sleeping space for a child, but many parents take a child to bed with them believing this is for the child's own good. In reality, the child may be a buffer between Mom and Dad or the parent is lonely and in need of a sleep partner. When children get out of their beds and consistently sleep with their parents, this is a sign of possible childhood trauma, and it needs to be investigated. If you had to share a bed, how do you feel about that? _____
Did you ever wish for your own bed? _____

19. If you slept with a parent on a regular basis, did you ever feel special? _____ Did you ever sleep with one parent while the other slept elsewhere? _____ If so, did you feel more important than the parent not sleeping in the parental bed? _____

20. Do you remember a time in your childhood when somebody touched you on your genitals or had you touch them on their genitals while in a bed? _____
If so, please describe the incident _____
_____
_____

How did you feel about the incident then? _____
_____

How do you feel about it now? _____
_____

21. If you do not remember an incident such as the above happening to you, but suspect it is a possibility, write out your reasoning for such suspicion (i.e., symptoms) _____
_____

22. Were you ever awakened late at night to be abused, lectured or harassed, or were you ever awakened by the disruptive behavior of an alcoholic or rageaholic parent, grandparent or sibling? _____ These are boundary violations. If so, describe the incidents

_____

_____

Your Room

23. Did your parents rarely check up on you in your room? _____ Do you believe you did not receive enough interested attention from your parents with regard to your activities in your room? _____ Do you wish your parents would have paid more attention to you and your activities? _____

24. Were you too free to do as you pleased in your room? _____ If so, how do you feel about this now? _____

Did you ever feel your parents were not interested in what you were doing in your room? _____

25. Were you allowed to decorate your own room as you pleased or were there guidelines for you? _____
If you had guidelines, do you feel they were appropriate or too rigid?_____
Did your room express your personality, or that of a parent or caretaker? _____ If it expressed your personality, describe how _____

If it described the personality of your parent or caretaker, describe how _____

How do you feel about that? _____

Did you like your room? _____ Tell why or why not _____

_____

Did your parents take an interest in how your room was decorated by being supportive and encouraging? _____ If not, how do you feel about that?

_____

_____

26. Did you have a bedtime curfew? _____ If so, do you believe it was reasonable? _____ If you didn't have a bedtime curfew, how do you feel about that?

_____

_____

Children need structure in their lives. If the structure is too rigid, it can stunt creativity and the development of healthy independence. If parents do not provide healthy structure, discipline, support and guidelines, children do not develop these necessary skills for successful living in adulthood. Healthy structure and guidelines teach us how to set boundaries with ourselves and others. Guidelines during childhood also provide us with a sense of security.
Do you feel you received the above? _____

27. Take a look at your answers to questions 1-26 and describe how they relate to the boundaries you have in your adult life _____

_____

_____

Are there any parallels? _____ Describe how your family of origin upbringing, with regards to your personal space in childhood, has affected you today

_____

_____

_____

28. What are the problem areas you need to address for your recovery and the development of healthy boundaries?

    a. _____

b. _____

c. _____

Do you promise yourself to explore these areas of difficulty? _____ If you said yes, *congratulations!* You are on your way to repairing your damaged boundaries.

29. Bathrooms are always an excellent gauge of a family system's boundaries. As mentioned earlier, some families are chaotic and others are rigid with respect to personal privacy. In chaotic family systems, people use one another's toothbrushes, combs, razors and makeup without asking — while in rigid families it is an unspoken rule that personal articles are never to be touched by anyone other than the owner. In families lacking in boundaries, privacy is unheard of. People walk in on one another while the toilet is in use or during bathing, seeing this as normal family behavior. In families with rigid barriers, family members are overly cautious with regards to every-day experiences such as bathing, using the toilet, nudity and so on. The following questions will allow you to explore the rules and boundaries your family followed with regard to the bathroom, and we also will examine how those childhood experiences continue to affect your boundaries today.

Your Bathroom

Did your family have rules and regulations for bathroom use? _____ If so, list rules (Example: lifting toilet seat for males, shutting door during use, cleaning up after self.)

a. _____

b. _____

c. _____

d. _____

e. _____

30. What is your earliest memory of the bathroom? (Bathing, toilet training, watching a parent bathe or shave.) _____
How do you feel about this memory? _____

31. How many bathrooms do you remember having in the house or houses you grew up in? _____ Did your parents have a bathroom separate from the children? _____ If so, were you ever allowed to use their bathroom? _____ If everybody shared one bathroom, did you have a drawer or place for your bathroom articles? _____

32. What were the family rules regarding use of the toilet? (i.e., having to shut the door, knocking to see if the bathroom was in use.) List three specific rules:

   1. _____
   2. _____
   3. _____

33. Did family members ever walk in on you unannounced while you were using the toilet? _____ If yes, what was your response to this and how did you feel? _____
Was this occurrence a rare one, regular or often?

34. (When my son, Aaron, turned two and a half, he began telling Michael and me to leave him alone when he would use the toilet. He also would close the door, setting a boundary with us which said he wanted to use the toilet by himself.) If your parents wanted to come into the bathroom and you were using it, were you able to say no? _____ If so, what was their response? _____

If not, what was your response? _____

35. Did your parents or siblings ever use the toilet in front of you? _____ How did you feel about this?

_____

_____

(I once walked into a boutique to do some shopping. The owner of the boutique excused herself and said she needed to use the restroom and continued talking with me on her way there. As she continued talking with me, she walked to the toilet and proceeded to use it with the door open while I was still standing outside. I was stunned, but she continued using the toilet in my presence as if this were normal procedure. This action told me a great deal about her family of origin and their boundaries.)

36. When a friend or relative or spouse uses the toilet in front of you today, how do you feel about this?

_____

Does it seem normal, uncomfortable or offensive?

_____

37. Do you use the toilet in front of others? _____

38. Are you overly cautious in your use of the toilet? _____ If so, how do you feel if someone accidentally walks in on you while you are using the bathroom? _____

39. In some families, parents are overly concerned with fecal material and urine, and have an overwhelming need for cleanliness. Some children are shamed or scolded for not wiping themselves properly or putting the toilet seat down. Did you have any of these experiences? _____ If so, describe them _____

_____

40. If your family was overly concerned with cleanliness, describe how that was acted out in your family system _____

_____

Did you ever feel as though urination or defecation were nasty, ugly, shameful behaviors to be hidden and not talked about? _____

41. This can affect us in adult life, setting us up to be fearful of germs or dirty things. Some of us can even become somewhat phobic of bathrooms in gas stations or restaurants or of our own bodily smells and excretions. Does the above relate to you at all? _____

42. What is your earliest memory of a bathing experience in childhood? _____
    Is this a pleasant or unpleasant memory? _____

43. At what age did your parents stop bathing you and allow you to bathe yourself? _____ When children reach age three to four, they are very capable of bathing themselves and usually ask to do so.

44. Do you remember which parent was the most responsible for seeing to it that you were bathed?
    _____

45. Did you ever bathe with a sibling or parent? _____
    If so, describe your experience _____
    _____

    After toddler age, it is sexually abusive for parents to bathe with children. Children need to be allowed personal space and privacy for bathing as it teaches them what privacy is and how to set boundaries. It also teaches them that it is all right for them to set boundaries for alone time in the bathroom.

46. At what age do you remember bathing yourself?
    _____

47. At what age were you no longer allowed to enter the bathroom while a parent was bathing? _____

48. At what age do you remember asking for privacy from parents and siblings during personal bathing time? _____

49. Did you ever receive enemas? _____ If so, how do you remember feeling during such an experience or experiences? _____

    _____

    (Enemas are an indirect form of sexual abuse and can produce feelings of invasion, powerlessness and shame. Enemas also can damage boundaries, and a sense of overwhelming powerlessness sets us up to have issues in adulthood around self-protection and care in interpersonal experiences and in sexual situations.)

50. Did you ever have a medical condition which involved manipulation of your genital area for medical examination or for the purposes of applying medication? _____ If so, describe the incident

    _____

    Describe how you felt about this _____

    _____

    (Excessive genital infections or rashes can be a symptom of childhood sexual trauma. Also medical procedures involving the genital areas during childhood are forms of indirect sexual abuse, even if they are necessary. These experiences produce feelings of shame, humiliation and powerlessness.)

51. If you have had experiences similar to those described in questions 49 or 50, please describe how these experiences are still impacting you in the here and now (i.e., fear of doctors, bladder or urethral infections, sexual difficulties.) _____

    _____

52. In adulthood how do your parents behave with their boundaries when they are using the toilet or bathroom for bathing or changing? _____

    _____

53. In adulthood, how do your parents behave boundary-wise when you are using the toilet, changing clothes or bathing? _____

_____

54. In adulthood, how do you behave boundary-wise when you are using the toilet, changing clothes or bathing? _____

_____

55. If you have children, how do you behave boundary-wise when they are using the toilet, changing clothes or bathing? _____

_____

(One of the first questions I will ask a new client is, "How was sex discussed in your family of origin?" or "Who told you about sex?" These loaded questions can provide immediate information about the boundaries one grew up with. So many of us have been indirectly sexually abused as a result of our parents' faulty sexual boundaries. As mentioned earlier, indirect sexual abuse means abuse which occurred in our families but was not done with intention by our caregivers. Indirect sexual abuse can set us up in adulthood not only to have confusion about sexual matters, but also to be lacking in clarity about our own sexual boundaries.)

Sex

56. Who told you about sex? _____ How was it presented to you by your parents? _____
Were you satisfied with this presentation? _____
If not, how come? _____

_____

57. How did your parents discuss sex in general with one another, siblings or in relationships toward pregnancy before marriage, premarital sex, homosexuality, etc.? _____

_____

Did they believe the above were sinful? _____

58. Did your parents have specific attitudes towards women who had sex before marriage? _____ If so, what were they? _____ What was their attitude towards males who had sex before marriage? _____

59. Were there restrictions around style of dress for you as an adolescent? (i.e., no short skirts or make-up; for males, no long hair or tight pants.) _____ Was dating controlled? (i.e., not allowed to date certain people from particular social backgrounds or ethnic groups.) _____

60. How old were you at the time of your first sexual experience? _____ Describe your experience _____ _____ How many sexual partners have you had in your lifetime? _____ Do you ever use sex to feel vali-dated, worthwhile or to change the way you feel? _____ If so, describe instances of this _____ _____

61. Do you like sex? _____ Do you feel like your sex-ual appetite is unusually excessive or less than nor-mal? _____ Have you ever been accused of being too sexual or frigid? _____ Do you have concerns about any of your sexual behavior? _____ If so, what concerns you? _____ Have you ever discussed this with a friend or a helping professional? _____ If not, it is suggested you find a therapist to talk to.

62. How did your parents feel about masturbation? _____ If you don't know, this indicates your parents had shame about the topic because it wasn't discussed. Who did talk to you about masturbating? _____ Describe the conversation _____ _____

Some people have been punished for masturbating. If this happened to you, describe the experience

_____

Do you masturbate today? _____ Do you feel it is excessive or too limited? _____ Do you use masturbation in place of your sexual relationship with your spouse or lover or to relieve painful feelings or when bored? _____ If so, you may be using sex addictively. If you do not masturbate at all, how do you feel about this? _____
This may be an indication of unresolved abuse.

63. If you are gay (homosexual or lesbian), how does your family feel about this? _____
Describe how they reacted when you first shared your sexual preference with them _____

_____

How did your father act specifically? _____

_____

How did your mother act specifically? _____

_____

How did your siblings react? _____

_____

Did you feel accepted, rejected, or is there just a "no talk" rule about your sexuality? _____ Do you feel totally comfortable with your sexuality? _____ Do you have shame, excessive fear of what others say or confusion about your sexuality? _____ If you do, I suggest you speak to a therapist who understands gay issues. If we are not comfortable with our sexuality, we have difficulty understanding boundaries.

64. If you are not gay, have you ever wondered at one time or another if you possibly were? _____ If the concern was during adulthood, this can be related to unresolved sexual abuse issues. Usually it is in response to being sexually abused by the same sex. Same-sexed abuse, as with opposite-sex abuse, causes a great deal of boundary blurring. Sexual

abuse, direct or indirect, can create a great deal of confusion around personal sexuality.

65. Can you say no to the sexual advances of another if you are not in the mood for sex, or do you engage in sexual encounters when you really don't want to? _____ If you said yes, how do you feel about this? _____

_____

Cite a recent example of such behavior _____

_____

If you are single, how soon after an initial meeting with another in dating situations do you find your-self engaging in sexual relationships? _____

_____

If you are married or in a significant relationship, have you ever found yourself engaging in sexual acts you find distasteful? _____ Describe a recent incident _____

_____

("What about the word *no* is it you do not under-stand, Carla?" was a phrase I heard from several close friends who had the courage to confront my inability to use this word. Many of us, when asked to do something by another, be it a spouse, child, relative or friend, have the word *no* on the tips of our tongues only to hear ourselves replying *yes*. As we listen to ourselves say yes to the requests of others over and over again when we do not want to, we kick ourselves and follow resentfully through with our commitment. As mentioned earlier, the ability to say *no* is acquired between the ages of 18 months and three years.)

The following are questions to help us sort out where our concepts of this word originated.

Basic Boundary Behavior

66. First of all, check any of the items below that you have difficulty saying no to:

_____ Requests for your services (making cakes
for a family gathering, fixing a relative's car,
giving a friend a ride, babysitting a relative's
or friend's child when you don't want to)

_____ Requests from others to borrow your personal belongings when you don't want to
lend them out

_____ Requests from others to borrow money
from you when you do not have extra money or don't feel like lending it out

_____ Invitations to events or gatherings you find
boring

_____ Sexual advances from spouse or lovers or
dating partners when you are not in the
mood

_____ Requests to participate in sexual activities
which feel emotionally or physically uncomfortable or which seem distasteful to you

_____ Touches, hugs or kisses offered by others
when you would rather not

_____ Gifts received from others which you feel
uncomfortable taking

_____ Offers of food or drink when you are not
hungry or thirsty

_____ Requests from others to listen to them,
even when you are not in the mood or have
something you need to be doing instead

_____ Phone calls from others when you are busy
or engaged in activity important to you

_____ Relatives who invite themselves over to
your home without asking

_____ Friends who invite themselves over to your
home without asking

_____ Relatives who invite themselves over to
your home for an overnight stay

_____ Friends who invite themselves for an overnight stay.

67. If you have a spouse or lover, are you able to say no to their requests when you do not want to fulfill them? _____

68. If you answered no, describe those requests you have difficulty saying no to _____
_____
_____

69. Do you ever say no to a request from a significant other, then find yourself fulfilling it anyway? ____

70. If you answered yes, describe these experiences
_____
_____
_____

71. Are you able to say no to your children's requests when you feel they are not appropriate? _____

72. Do you feel like you have to explain yourself for your decisions? _____

73. Do you ever say no to your children only to give in later? _____

74. If you answered yes, describe some instances of this behavior _____
_____

75. Have you ever been told you are "a pushover," "too easy" or been accused of spoiling your kids? _____

76. How do you feel about your parenting skills and ability to set healthy limits with your children?
_____
_____
_____

77. Have you ever been accused of being "too rigid," "too strict" or "too controlling" with your children? _____

78. If so, describe times when this has happened _____
_____
_____

   Most of us parent one of two ways: with little or no boundaries at all or with rigid uncompromising rules. Both are in the extreme, dysfunctional and a product of our own upbringing and how the word no was presented to us.

79. Do you remember saying no to your parents while growing up? _____ Think back in your childhood and remember how your mother responded to you when you said no. Describe what happened _____
_____
_____

80. Describe what happened when you said no to your father _____
_____
_____

81. Some children are punished for saying no to their parents. If you were punished, you were discouraged from learning how to set boundaries. If you were punished with emotional withdrawal, ignoring behavior, physical hitting or verbal reprimand, please describe these abuses _____
_____
_____

82. How did you feel about these incidences then? _____
_____

83. How do you feel about it now? _____
_____

84. Are you fearful of rejection, abandonment or punishment for saying no to friends and relatives today
as an adult? _____

85. If so, can you relate these fears to any childhood
experiences? If so, describe them and how they are
related to today's experiences _____

_____

_____

(We also learn how to use the word no by watching our parents. As mentioned earlier, the adult
women in my family of origin had great difficulty
using the word no. As a consequence, it never
occurred to me to refuse the requests of others. I
truly believed I did not have a choice and that, if
asked, my only option was to follow through and
comply.)

86. Do you feel your mother had difficulty saying no to
the requests of your father, relatives, neighbors,
co-workers, yourself or your siblings? _____ If so,
describe instances of this _____

_____

_____

87. Did your father have difficulty saying no to your
mother, in-laws, his parents, friends, neighbors,
you or your siblings? _____ If so, describe instances of this _____

_____

_____

88. Sometimes it was easier for my parents to say no to
the neighbors or co-workers, but more difficult
with family members. Were there particular people
either of your parents had difficulty saying no to?

_____

_____

89. For us as adults, we find it is easier to say no to some as opposed to others. List those people you have difficulty saying no to (relatives, friends, co-workers, etc.) _____

_____

_____

90. Do any of the above listed have similar physical characteristics, common behavioral patterns or other similar characteristics in common? (For example, I had difficulty with men who had strong personalities and who were loud. I found it difficult to say no to such individuals because they were intimidating.)

_____

_____

91. When someone is behaving in a particular way (such as — like a victim, a tyrant or a whiner), do you find it more difficult to say no to their requests? _____
If yes, describe this _____

_____

92. With the information gathered from questions 89, 90 and 91, examine what it is you need to do in order to be able to say no to others, such as do family of origin work, assertiveness training or anger work with a therapist to reclaim your power. (When I was around those individuals who had abused me in my youth or when I was in the company of those having characteristics similar to those who abused me, I lost my power to say no. I had to work through my own abuse issues to learn how to feel my own power and say no when necessary, regardless of the personality.)
List your plan of action for learning how to say no:

    a. I will _____

    b. I will _____

    c. I will _____

93. Are you committed to following through on this plan? _____ If so, congratulations! You are beginning to reclaim yourself! It is most important for us to learn that when we say no to others in order to take care of ourselves, we are not being selfish, self-centered or ungrateful. What we are doing is being adults who are aware that we are responsible for our own well-being and that it is our job to take care of ourselves.

Emotional Incest

94. Many of us grew up in families full of emotional incest. As we discussed earlier, many of us had relationships with adults during childhood which placed us in the roles of "Daddy's Little Princess," "Mama's Little Man," "Father's Caretaker" or "Mother's Protector." These roles set us up to take care of others in adulthood. Many of us, as a result of the emotional incest in our families of origin, are still emotionally taking care of one or more of our relatives today.

Let's look at JoAnne's story.

JoAnne and her father had a special relationship. When JoAnne's father came home from work, he and JoAnne would go into the backyard to talk. At these times JoAnne's father would always have a small gift of chocolate or a toy for her and he would share with her his day at the office. JoAnne loved the attention she received, even though she did not understand half of what her father was talking about. All that office stuff was very confusing, but she gave her father delighted attention anyway. When JoAnne went away to college, her father would call to share with her what his life was like. JoAnne would become irritated with her father's lack of interest in her own life. She would pretend to listen while cleaning her dorm room or while watching television, relieved at the end of the conversation.

When JoAnne married, she was still receiving phone calls several times a week from her father. Busy with her two children and husband, she resented her father's need for her time, but knew she never could say anything, for she was all he had to share with. She hated taking care of her father emotionally in this way and would find herself taking her frustrations out on her children or husband by raging after phone calls from her father. At times she would accuse her husband of demanding too much of her time as her father did. JoAnne felt confused and overwhelmed, and was full of fear the day her mother died because she knew that now her father would be even more needy.

Did you have a special relationship with a parent, grandparent or other adult during your childhood? _____ If so, who was this adult and describe the relationship _____

_____

_____

95. Did this relationship make you feel more grown up? _____ Did this relationship make you behave in a more grown-up manner? _____ If so, how?

_____

_____

Have You Been Overempowered?

96. For those of us who have been overempowered with emotionally incestuous relationships, it is often difficult to see how we have been abused. The following are characteristics of an overempowered individual. Check those that apply to you:

_____ Difficulty expressing anger, sadness or loneliness

_____ A deep sense of loneliness

_____ Usually self-sufficient ("I'll do it myself")

_____ Difficulty in asking for help

_____ Strong need to appear in control to others

_____ Strong need for perfection

_____ In a caretaking career in adulthood

_____ Fearful of intimacy or opening up honestly to others

_____ Difficulty communicating in healthy ways with the same sex or opposite sex

_____ Does a lot of listening in relationships and has difficulty getting emotional needs met

_____ Gets "dumped on" with the problems of others

_____ Feels obligated to be available for one or both parents, siblings, etc., whenever needed or plays parent or sibling counselor or caretaker on a regular basis at the expense of self, current spouse or relationship or children

_____ Has difficulty setting limits with parental or sibling requests; has difficulty saying no to relatives

_____ Marriage or relationship partner has complained about the demands of in-laws or other relatives

_____ You defend your family's behavior to your partner

_____ Ever feel grandiose or so powerful that you could change history all by yourself, or do you ever feel responsible for events and situations which are beyond your control?

_____ When you feel out of control, you get scared, panicked or rage to regain control

_____ Have difficulty taking responsibility for behaviors which are offensive to others, even when confronted

_____ Ever feel you are responsible for your parents' or mate's happiness?

_____ Ever feel as though you could change the course of history in another person's life, like sober up an alcoholic or addict, cure someone's emotional pain or fix another's life situation?

Overempowered individuals tend to be over-controlling, over-responsible and tend to be attracted to people they can fix and rescue because in childhood they were set up to take care of others emotionally and even physically.

(Michael was an overempowered child who grew into an adult who believed it was his job to relieve me of my addictions. When his efforts failed, he felt like a failure.)

Most overempowered children have been emotionally incested and set up to meet the needs of one or both parents. And this type of abuse is usually indirect. Because of this, it is difficult for overempowered adults to realize they have been abused. It is impossible for overempowered individuals to have healthy boundaries and successful relationships until they learn how to set boundaries with their family of origin. For some, this even involves emotionally divorcing the parent who has set up the emotionally incestuous relationship and re-establishing a relationship with that parent consisting of healthy boundaries and the word no when necessary and appropriate. By resolving those issues of overempowerment where they originated in childhood, there are benefits which not only greatly improve our relationships with members of our family of origin, but also spill over into our relationships with others.

97. If you have been abused by a special relationship with an adult in childhood or as a consequence of overempowerment, describe it _____

98. Describe how the above continues to affect you in your relationships today _____

99. List what it is you need to do to resolve your over-empowered behavior (i.e., therapy, treatment, family of origin workshops, 12-Step meetings, such as Co-dependents Anonymous, Al-Anon, Adult Children of Alcoholics) _____

100. If you have made a decision to explore your history as an overempowered child, I really congratulate you. This is one of the most difficult of family of origin issues to explore because there was a payoff for it. This payoff was special attention. Even though it felt good at times, many of us have paid a big price for those strokes and continue to do so in adulthood. What is your payoff today (i.e., feeling powerful, receiving attention, feeling special)? _____

Congratulations on your honesty!

Fear of Abandonment

Another feeling which sets us up to have difficulty setting boundaries in adulthood is an overwhelming fear of abandonment. Usually this feeling has its origins in our youth and is in response to some unresolved trauma. Whenever children are emotionally, physically or sexually abused, they are also being abandoned because their well-being is being totally ignored. In adulthood, some of us allow ourselves to be abused by others and do not confront such behavior for fear of being abandoned. It is as if it is easier for us to accept the abuse more than to experience possible abandonment by confronting such behavior. The following are questions to help us determine if our own fears of abandonment interfere with our ability to set limits with others.

101. Think about the times you have given in to the requests of others when you did not want to. At any of these times were you fearful of saying no because you were afraid they would not like you? _____ If so, describe some of these situations

_____

_____

102. Have you ever accepted hostile, discounting or shaming remarks from another and not defended yourself for fear they would end the relationship or leave you? _____ If so, describe this _____

_____

103. Have you ever wanted to confront someone on their behavior which was offensive to you but did not because you were fearful of their reactions? _____ If yes, what reaction were you afraid of?

_____

Describe your situations _____

_____

104. Are you fearful of confronting your parents, siblings or relatives about their behaviors because you fear being ignored, abandoned, rejected, raged at or shamed? _____ If yes, describe how each of the following would react if you confronted them, said no to them or set limits on their behavior or demands:

    a. Mother _____

    b. Father _____

    c. Brother _____

    d. Sister _____

    e. Grandparent _____

    f. Grandparent _____

    g. Aunt _____

    h. Uncle _____

    i. Others _____

105. Are you fearful of confronting your mate, children, friends or co-workers for fear of being ignored, abandoned, rejected, raged at or shamed? _____
If yes, describe how the following people would react to your setting boundaries with them or confronting them:

   a. Spouse, lover _____

   b. Child _____

   c. Child _____

   d. Friend _____

   e. Friend _____

   f. Co-worker _____

   g. Boss _____

106. Do you see any similarities between 104 and 105? _____ If yes, what are they? _____
_____
_____

107. Are you fearful of being alone? _____ If so, what scares you the most about being alone? _____
_____

108. Do you ever feel God has abandoned you or that there really isn't a God? _____ This is a typical reaction to childhood abandonment. I have not met one atheist yet who didn't have severe abandonment issues in childhood.

109. Do you abandon yourself, your desires, wishes and goals to be available to others so that they will not leave you? _____ Do you know that in order to learn how to set boundaries with others, we must first learn how to not abandon ourselves?

110. Many of us abandon our emotional, physical, sexual and spiritual needs to be available to others in fear of being abandoned. As a consequence of this, we

do not set boundaries with others. How do you see that you abandon yourself in order to take care of others? List three ways you do this:

a. _____

b. _____

c. _____

111. Where do you believe your fear of abandonment originated? _____

_____

112. How do you see the above influencing your life today? _____

_____

113. What do you need to do to begin not abandoning yourself? _____

_____

114. Some of us are so fearful of abandonment, we need outside assistance, such as therapy, to work through these issues. If you are in need of outside assistance, what are you willing to do? _____

_____

115. When will you do the above? _____
You have just contracted with yourself to resolve your abandonment fears. I wish you well on your journey!

Triangulation

116. Another dynamic which causes us difficulty in our ability to set boundaries with family members and others is the triangulation or being the "go between" for two other people. Boundaries are not only confusing in this situation, but usually nonexistent. Look at the following diagrams and plot the triangles you are currently involved in.

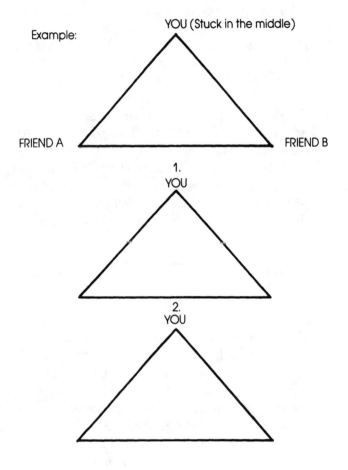

Figure 9.1. Your Triangle Can Involve
Friends, Relatives, Children, Spouse, Etc.

117. How do you feel when involved in triangles (mad, glad, sad, empowered, special, needed)? _____

118. If you have been involved in triangles, describe your role (the go-between, the message-sender or the message-receiver) _____

119. Have you ever found yourself in trouble or in sticky situations as a consequence of being involved in a triangle? _____

120. Do you ever remember your parents using you as a "go-between" for them? For example: "Tell your mother I'm angry with her . . . Tell your father to pick up the laundry . . . Tell your father I'm not going out tonight; I have a cold . . . Tell your mother to go to the doctor . . . Tell your father to get a new suit." If so, describe the types of messages you heard _____

   a. _____

   b. _____

   c. _____

121. Do you ever find yourself listening to one of your parents complain about the other or about another relative or friend? _____ If so, do you find yourself ever giving advice? _____ Have you ever found yourself in an uncomfortable situation because of your advice-giving? _____ Or from getting involved with the problems of another's relationship? _____ If so, describe this _____

122. Triangulation is learned in childhood. It gives us a sense of power to be included and involved in the lives of others, but sometimes our involvement can backfire with both parties angry with us. Also triangulation can become emotionally exhausting and frustrating. Some of us fear being left out of the

action, so to speak, and involve ourselves in triangulation from the fear of being abandoned. Describe examples listed above which have happened in your life _____

_____

123. What is your payoff for being involved in triangles? _____
Is it worth it? _____ If not, how come? _____

_____

124. There are several things you can do to avoid triangulation. You can . . .
    a. Tell the other person you care about them but do not wish to get in the middle of their relationship problems.
    b. Tell the other person that if they have something to say to someone else, they probably need to share it with them instead of you.
    c. Tell them that you don't feel comfortable delivering messages for them.
    d. Tell them if they want to know how your friend is doing, they might want to call him or her.
    e. Tell them if they are angry with the other person, they need to tell them.
    f. Tell them you care for both of them and do not wish to take sides.
    g. Tell them you have got yourself into trouble by being in the middle before and choose not to do this again.

It is also important for us to be aware of when we are setting others up to carry our messages. (The last time I tried to set one of my sisters up to carry a message to the other during a phone conversation, she threatened to hang the phone up. I was so used to being involved in triangles that I found myself unconsciously passing information on to my other sister. I was amazed at how natural this felt and had to examine why I did not want to relay my message myself.) Many times we feel safer having our messages relayed for us, fearing the reaction of the receiver. If this is the case, we need to examine why.

If there have been instances in your life of triangulation, list one and what you could have told the person in order to stop the triangulation _____

_____

125. If you have been one to set another up to pass messages in triangles, take a look at why it has not felt safe for you to be direct. What were your fears?

_____

_____

126. In order for us to develop healthy boundaries it is important for us not to participate in triangulation. For the next week observe how many triangles you are involved in and examine them by drawing diagrams and describe the situations and participants.

SUNDAY   Brief description _____

_____

_____

_____

_____

_____

MONDAY   Brief description _____

_____

_____

_____

_____

TUESDAY   Brief description _____
_____
_____
_____
_____

WEDNESDAY   Brief description _____
_____
_____
_____
_____

THURSDAY   Brief description _____
_____
_____
_____
_____

FRIDAY   Brief description _____
_____
_____
_____
_____

SATURDAY   Brief description _____
_____
_____
_____
_____

What did you discover? _____
_____

What role are you usually in (sender, messenger, receiver)? _____
How do you feel about your participation in triangles now? _____
_____

127. Is the payoff for your participation worth it? ____

128. What are your fears about pulling out of the triangles you are involved in? _____
_____

129. It is important to address these behaviors in order to begin establishing healthy boundaries. Triangulation stunts honesty, true intimacy and healthy conflict resolution in relationships. What do you feel is necessary for you to do to begin addressing your participation in triangles? (Examine family of origin for source of behavior, contract with self to not triangulate, seek therapy, etc.) _____
_____

130. It is difficult to avoid triangulation, and in many situations others are not too pleased with us when we stop our participation. Triangulation also is a form of caretaking. (As long as my sister was carrying messages from me to my other sister, she was caretaking by not holding me responsible for delivering my own messages. When she first set a boundary and said no to my request, I was angry with her for not taking care of me. "How dare she!" I thought, until I realized my request was violating her boundaries.)
    Describe your feelings if anyone has stopped you when you were attempting to triangulate _____
_____

Dealing With Anger

In many situations our fears of setting boundaries or saying no are about our fears of the reactions of others. A number of us have difficulty with another being angry with us. Some of us even freeze up when confronted with the anger of another. This response usually has its source in our family of origin and is a consequence of our parents' behavior surrounding the emotion of anger. Fearing the angry responses of others can set the stage for dysfunctional boundaries. Let's take a look at how our family of origin dealt with anger by completing questions 131 through 151:

131. When my father was angry, he _____
_____

132. I knew my father was angry when _____
_____

133. I feared my father's anger because _____
_____

134. When my father was angry with me, he would ___
_____

135. The most angry I ever saw my father was _____
_____

136. He behaved in the following ways _____
_____

137. During this time I felt _____
_____

138. When my mother was angry, she _____
_____

139. I knew my mother was angry when _____
_____

140. I feared my mother's anger because _____

_____

141. When my mother was angry with me, she would

_____

_____

142. The most angry I ever saw my mother was when

_____

_____

143. During this time I felt _____

_____

144. When I am confronted by an angry person, I react
by _____

_____

145. When I am angry, I _____

_____

146. When I am confronted by an angry person, I feel

_____

_____

147. When I am angry at others, their responses have
been _____

_____

148. When I tell my father I am angry with him, he

_____

_____

149. When I tell my mother I am angry with her, she

_____

_____

150. How are your mother's and father's behavior with
anger during your childhood still affecting you today in your relationships and in your ability to set
healthy boundaries? List three consequences:

a. _____

b. _____

c. _____

151. Most of us fear our own anger and stuff it, never allowing it to surface. Others of us explode and rage, offending those around us. How do you express your anger? _____

Healthy expression of anger involves owning it, admitting it and working through it as it surfaces. Most of us do not know that the following phrases are not only healthy but healing:

- "I'm angry with you because . . ."
- "I'm angry that didn't go the way I thought it would."
- "I'm angry my childhood was so rotten."
- "I'm angry with my spouse, children, parents, boss, because . . ."
- "I'm angry you're not there for me."
- "I'm angry I've abandoned myself."
- "I'm angry I don't know how to set boundaries with you."
- "I'm angry that you violated my boundaries."
- "I'm angry you expect me to fix you."
- "I'm angry that you are triangulating."

Stuffing our anger until we rage or get sick emotionally or physically is a display of unhealthy boundaries. Dealing with our anger in healthy ways as it comes up by talking about it, by doing rage work in therapy, by discussing it in a 12-Step meeting, by writing about it, by sharing it with the person we are angry with or by taking a plastic baseball bat to a stack of pillows allows us to begin experiencing our own anger.

When we can have our own anger in healthy ways, we slowly learn that another's anger will not kill us. I always thought the anger of others would destroy me and did whatever it took with people-pleasing behavior to avoid this. Today it is not uncommon at one time or another for my husband, child, relatives, friends, co-workers or peers to be angry with me for my behavior, be it appropriate or inappropriate or when I set boundaries. Being angry with one another is not only normal but healthy.

When we express our anger towards one another, we are building healthy intimacy and boundaries by saying, "I care about you enough to be honest and say . . ." and "I care about our relationship enough to share how dissatisfied I am with . . ." Learning how to confront the *anger* bogeyman begins by examining what we learned about anger in our family of origin, then deciding whether what we learned was healthy and if we choose to hang onto those beliefs or if we need to let go and develop our own.

Healthy anger allows us to take care of ourselves and it allows others to do the same. When we decide to begin to establish healthy boundaries, we are bound to experience anger from those around us who have difficulty with our new way of living. To say that all around us are going to be happy with our new way of being is ridiculous.

(I thought everyone would be pleased as punch that I was giving up my membership card to victims anonymous and taking care of myself in healthy responsible ways. I was way off base and began to realize that as in all things in life there are consequences to change. Some of the consequences to my new boundaries were not only surprising, but unexpected and confusing.)

Now I Have Boundaries, Why Is Everyone So Upset? | 10

"I'm not being a victim any-
more. Why is everyone so angry with me? I'm self-reliant,
not acting like a martyr. So how come people are frightened of me? I quit triangulating and lost a bunch of friends!
WHY? Isn't this supposed to be healthy for my recovery?
If these are boundaries and this is recovery, why are my
friends acting so strange towards me? Everybody kept telling me to learn how to have my feelings and set limits,
well, now I am and everyone is avoiding me."

How often have I heard the above and even said these
phrases myself, while wondering why having boundaries
was causing so much upheaval in my relationships with
family, friends and colleagues. Before recovery from addiction and family of origin unfinished business, I had
several characteristics with which all who knew me were
quite familiar. Even in my early years of recovery my
behavior was very predictable to those who knew me well.

I rarely had an opinion for fear of disagreeing with
another and always said yes to the requests of others,

fearful of losing their friendship with the word *no*. I was very agreeable in a syrupy people-pleasing sort of way and was available 24 hours every day for the concerns, problems and difficulties of others. I not only gave of myself emotionally in a co-dependent way on a regular basis, but was also in the habit of giving excessively of my material possessions to anybody who asked. Although I was constantly surrounded by people, I still felt abandoned and alone.

Learning To Set Limits

As I began to learn about boundaries, several things began to change in my life. The biggest change, of course, occurred within me and in my behavior. When people would call, I began setting limits with myself as to how much time I was willing to spare to sit and listen to problems. In order to get off the phone, I would periodically use excuses, such as, "The doorbell is ringing . . . I have to go to the bathroom . . . I'm just walking out the door," fearful of being truthful and saying, "I don't have four hours of listening time to spare today." Even though these excuses were little white lies, they gave me the opportunity to begin setting boundaries with others.

I eventually was able to honestly say, "I only have 10 minutes to give to you at this time," when called by those who were in need of my attention. Moving from providing four to five hours of phone attention to 10 to 20 minutes upset a number of people in my life. Slowly many of them stopped calling. I was crushed! I realized that as long as I was not willing to give, give, give, certain people in my life were going to leave me. My fears of abandonment set in, and I had to return once again to my family of origin unfinished business and grieve. I had to grieve the fact that I had grown up believing that as long as I gave, gave, gave, people would not leave me. It saddened me to see how I was repeating this pattern in adulthood, and I began to realize that I attracted people who had difficulty being emotionally available for me in the way I was available to them. I saw that I had set other people up to depend on me so that I would feel needed.

Learning To Say No

Another boundary I began to set involved the word *no*. In my profession, it is common for many of us to participate in community forums, presenting talks on mental health issues to church, school and business groups. For years I had been a very popular speaker because I always said yes, even when exhausted or when my schedule was overloaded. I rarely said no and would provide these services free of charge, believing it must be my duty to educate the masses. While performing such duties, I would feel resentful, overwhelmed and usually unappreciated. I would say to myself, "Don't they see what I am doing for them?"

At the same time my need to be needed, stemming from childhood, was being fulfilled once again at the expense of myself. When I began to realize what it was I was doing and how I was responsible for being overloaded, I decided to start setting limits by saying no to some of these invitations. The consequences of saying no were varied. Some were most understanding with comments such as, "It's good to see you taking care of yourself," but others responded with, "You think you're too good to speak to our group for free, don't you, Carla? Remember where you came from!"

Those who supported me in my need to take care of myself had validated my new desire for self-care and were appreciated for their understanding. What was so confusing were the responses of those who were angry with me for setting limits. In despair I would reply, "I'm taking care of myself. It has nothing to do with not being supportive of you or your organization. Nor do I think I'm too good, as you say, to speak at your function. I just need to set limits!" Many still did not understand my new behavior. They had been used to me being available at all times. One organization was used to calling me with a half hour's notice, knowing I would agree to speak as always.

I discovered that change for many was difficult and that I was responsible for setting up the pattern of always being available. This is what those around me had become used to. As I continued to set limits, rumors and unpleasant comments began to circulate and once again I felt abandoned, realizing how my need to be needed from childhood had repeated itself in adulthood.

Learning To Have And Express An Opinion

The greatest uproar in my recovery occurred when I began to honestly express myself. For years and years and years I had never really voiced an opinion because I never really thought I had any. And when I did have an opinion about a topic or situation, I kept it to myself for fear of upsetting others. Slowly I began saying things like:

- "I disagree with that."
- "I choose not to do this."
- "I'm sorry, but *no.*"
- "Please don't hug me today."
- "I don't want to talk with you right now about that."
- "Even though you don't like her, I do."
- "Just because you enjoy his company doesn't necessarily mean I do."
- "I didn't like that movie."
- "I don't want to eat here."
- "I agree to disagree."

One evening Michael and I went out to eat. I like my meat well done and always order it this way. The restaurant we were at was a Texas steak house and when asked how I would like my steak cooked, I replied, "Well done." The steak I received was so raw, in my opinion, it could have said "Moo!" I was not pleased at all, as I thought I had made myself very clear about my need for "well-done" meat. I looked at Michael in dismay and said, "I can't eat this. I'm going to send it back."

Michael looked shocked, as this was a whole new side of his wife he had never seen. Looking on in fear, he watched as I flagged our waiter down and shared my complaint. The waiter appeared disinterested with my concern, telling me this was the only way to eat this meat. I persisted in my quest for well-done meat as Michael slowly sank under the table. He was not used to watching me assert myself and he was embarrassed with my new behavior. I could not believe his response to my need to take care of myself by expressing dissatisfaction with my meal. At one point he even said, "Don't create such a scene," as he looked around the restaurant to see who was listening to my complaint. He added with a mortified look, "Here comes your food, now just eat it!"

Well, my meat was still raw! I could not believe how hard being a grown-up was as I once again waved to the waiter and told him about my inability to enjoy raw meat. Michael was beside himself, and I became angry with him for not being more supportive. Needless to say, I eventually received my steak cooked to my satisfaction and Michael and I had a huge fight in the parking lot.

Michael was not the only family member to have difficulty with the new me. Family members would say, "Carla, you used to be so sweet and agreeable! What has happened? You were such a pleasure to be around. Now we don't know what to expect from you."

When I began saying no to family members, their responses ranged from, "What have we done wrong?" to "But you used to always say yes before!" It was also difficult for family to understand my new boundaries because my behavior in recovery was completely opposite that of previous years.

For some time life within the family was rocky and several members found themselves in treatment, therapy and support groups in response to the boundaries my recovery had enabled me to set. I had moved from being the "identified patient," "caretaker" and "problem resolver" in my family to a grown-up woman who was vocal about her ideas, values and beliefs. Many family members and friends, including myself, were not prepared for the changes which accompanied my new role. It forced uncomfortable change and, in some cases, painful growth onto almost everyone involved. None could have predicted the changes which occurred as a result of my recovery.

Learning To Stay Out Of Triangles

Triangulation as a means of communication for me also had to be examined. I had played all three roles of sender, relayer and receiver throughout my life and had been victimized by many and had also victimized others. I made a decision to stop this form of communication in my life by first asking those in recovery with an understanding of triangulation to confront me when I was using this dysfunctional mode of communication. Secondly, if I found myself being triangulated by another, I immediately would talk about how uncomfortable I felt with it. By having others confront me on my inappropriate communicating, I was being held accountable for my behavior which violated the boundaries of close friends and family. This was difficult because I was having to look at those behaviors of mine which caused pain for others. I was having to own a side of myself I had ignored for years.

Confronting others when I felt I was being triangulated was also difficult. For years I had agreed to being triangulated by involving myself in the disputes of many. I felt needed at these times and was provided with a strong sense of power and control. But I had begun to realize that by being in between the difficulties of others, I was in many cases in the direct line of fire. Instead of the two in dispute directing their angry feelings towards one another, I was regularly saddled with their misdirected anger and grief.

With my new boundaries I began saying, "Please share your concern about her with her . . . If you are worried about him, please call him . . . No, I will not tell her that for you." Did I ever stir up a hornet's nest with this new behavior!!! I heard comments like, "Carla, you really don't care about this situation because if you really did, you would stay involved. You just don't love me anymore. You really are mean!"

For so many years relatives, friends and peers had depended on me to participate in triangles and now I was saying no. In my need to be needed I had agreed to participate many years back and had established many of these triangles in my life. To suddenly pull out forced me into examining my concepts of healthy communication and in some instances forced those in my life I had communicated for to communicate with one another.

What a frightening change that was! Without me to triangulate I was no longer needed and my abandonment fears kicked in once again. Frightened and not as needed, I realized I did not know who Carla was. I found I had been so caught up in the lives of others, I didn't know what I wanted to do, what I liked or what my life was really all about. My whole identity involved being needed and by setting boundaries, I realized I wasn't as needed by others as I thought I was.

Learning To Discover Who I Am

I discovered I had recreated those situations familiar to me from my family of origin which gave me purpose, identity and a reason to live all over again in my adult life. My new boundaries were forcing me to explore myself and discover who I was. I never expected this consequence and remember saying, "I don't even know if I like myself!" In my loneliness I cried to my Higher Power, "What do I do now? I feel so lonely! Nobody needs me!" Then I heard a voice from deep within say, "Carla, I need you! Quit abandoning me! Get to know me."

I eventually discovered I needed to take some quality time to discover who Carla was. For several years I avoided close relationships with others so that I could learn how to love myself. Even Michael was forced to do some growing as I finally got out of his way and quit stunting his growth with my dysfunctional caretaking behavior. I would take myself to the beach, write myself letters, go to movies and restaurants I enjoyed, and at times just sit in the back yard under a tree and enjoy being with me! It felt very strange at first, being with me, but eventually my time with me was special and treasured.

Learning To Set Boundaries

By learning how to set boundaries with others, I had opened up more opportunities for self-growth and exploration. I now had enough quiet time, without all the past caretaking of others, to explore my own creative and spiritual self. For years when I would look at myself in the mirror, I felt very disconnected from the person reflected back to me. I felt so out of touch with her and even a little frightened of her, too. Today when I look at her, I am confident that I know almost all of her. I know her wonderfully creative spiritual side which brims with compassion and goodwill and I also know that side of her which has tantrums periodically, making unrealistic impatient demands on not only herself, but on occasion the world.

I had to learn how to embrace all of Carla and love her. Some days I am quite pleased with Carla, her progress in recovery, the accomplishments in her life and with her adjustment to being a grown up. On other days, I truly am disappointed with her violating behavior, her manipulations and lack of patience.

Learning how to have boundaries forced me to grow up and accept responsibility for all of my behavior. By being responsible for all of *me* I discovered I was responsible not only for my recovery, but my life.

Boundaries also provided a new sense of freedom. I no longer had to avoid certain life experiences for fear of being victimized. Now I had tools to protect myself with and was responsible for allowing others to victimize me by not saying no or stating my position.

I also know I am going to continue to experience some consequences to the boundaries I set with others and that not everybody is going to be supportive, pleased or understanding. When these unpleasant consequences occur, it is necessary for me to seek out those who, like me, are continuing to work on the establishment of healthy boundaries. With this support I feel a sense of validation and belonging to a group whose primary purpose is to "grow up." Even those parts of me which will forever remain childlike are pleased that I am finally taking responsibility for their safety and well-being by setting limits with others.

Today fewer people call me on the phone, but those who do are close true friends who understand healthy sharing. They know when I set time limits, it is not a personal issue directed at them but my need to care for myself. One friend I call on a regular basis tells me up front whether or not she can talk and I do the same with her. When either of us cannot talk, the other respects this and feels comfortable with this type of honesty. Neither feels used or abused as the boundaries are always very clear and up front.

There are still those community organizations that have difficulty with me when I say no to their invitations. This is a natural consequence to setting such boundaries. To expect that all will be happy when I say no is not very realistic. But it is important for me to be at peace with myself. To say yes when I mean no promotes resentment towards those making the requests and sets me up to abandon and betray myself. Understanding the price I paid in the past for self-betrayal makes dealing with some of the negative consequences to my no's easier to accept.

Learning To Be Myself

By voicing my opinions, ideas, beliefs, values, needs and wants today, I can let those around me know where I stand. No longer do I have to sit and feel victimized, resentful and misunderstood because I have not let others know how I feel or what it is I need. Being silent gave me a license to be a martyr and victim. Today, as a grown-up, this type of behavior is not acceptable. My inner self feels angry when I allow this to happen because at these times I am not practicing self-care. Expressing my needs is difficult on occasion, especially when I risk experiencing the upset responses of others. But the pain of not taking care of myself by expressing my opinions, needs and values is much more difficult than the consequences of not doing so.

By not participating in triangles, I was forced to confront my own fears about conflict, disagreement, confrontation and intimacy. Being such a people-pleaser, I feared confrontation. By having someone else relay my messages for me, I never had to deal with the direct feelings of others. By being direct with my communication, I had to take responsibility for myself, my feelings and my messages. Some of the relationships I had been in for years could not withstand the directness of the communication involved and these relationships dissolved. I had to grieve them and the loss of my role within those relationships. In others, conflict ensued and although it was hard at the beginning, in the end, the relationships were more solid and honest.

Today, when eating out, I still send my meals back if I'm not satisfied. Michael still cringes a bit when I do so, but periodically now will do the same if not happy with what he has ordered.

The first time he returned a plate to the restaurant kitchen, I was in total shock for a week. When he told the waitress he was dissatisfied, I replied with, "Well, I just can't believe this! You're sending something back after all the flack you've given me!" He explained, "Well, I decided if you could do it, I could do it, too." We do learn so much from each other along this path called recovery!!

The most important person in each of our lives is not our spouses or lovers, children or relatives, friends or peers, it's ourselves. Many of us fear knowing ourselves because we are afraid we will not like what we see if we allow ourselves the time and space necessary for self-discovery. So we occupy ourselves with the problems and concerns of others or we block ourselves off from who we really are with addiction and distractions of all kinds. Fearful of intimacy with ourselves, we avoid learning who we are at all costs.

It is impossible to live life to the fullest as long as we are running from who we really are. By stopping ourselves and saying, "Hey, who are you really?" we begin a most exciting adventure, full of drama, excitement, joy and the blossoming growth self-discovery provides. To risk knowing ourselves takes a great deal of courage, persistence

and — most of all — honesty. Though initially the beginning journey is fear-producing, painful and at times very
lonely, the benefits involve true inner peace, feeling cen-
tered, confident with a comfortable self-acceptance which
can only be described as true spirituality.

Learning To Let Others Grow

Sometime back I received a phone call from a friend
who was in great emotional pain. As she talked I felt
enormous compassion for her and her situation, but knew
that all I could offer was support. After describing her
most difficult situation to me, she asked, "Tell me what to
do! If you really care for me you will tell me what to do!"
I sadly shared with her that as her friend it was not my
place to tell her what to do. Once again she said, "If you
really cared about me, you would tell me what to do." I
replied, "It is because I care so much for you that I cannot
tell you what to do."

Most of us confuse compassionate support with dysfunctional caretaking. When we caretake, we are in a
position of power, which is usually not in the best interest
of whomever we are sharing with. We also compromise
ourselves during caretaking because we are assuming
another's responsibility which is not ours. We stunt not
only the growth of others through caretaking and enabling
behavior, but also cut off our own chances for growth
and self-exploration. By allowing others to cross and violate our boundaries, we enable them in their violating
behaviors. By violating the boundaries of others with inappropriate behaviors and caretaking, we are being irres-
ponsible to ourselves and to them.

Our first reponsibility is to ourselves and our own
growth. By being focused in on abstaining from our addictive behaviors, resolving our unfinished childhood family of origin business, establishing our own healthy boundaries and dealing effectively with the consequences of our
boundaries, we are demonstrating one of the highest
forms of self-love and love for others. When we have our
addictions in check, our unfinished business straight and

our boundaries out front, we can be available to our spouses, family and friends with healthy support and compassion and we can model for our own children healthy self-love and acceptance in adulthood.

It is my hope for you, the reader, that you will take the courageous path of self-exploration and continue your brave journey towards discovering who you really are. I am grateful that you have chosen this book as one of the many tools to accompany you on your journey.

I believe we all have an individual path to follow and specific journey in this life to complete. Unfortunately, many of us have difficulty recognizing our path or can't see we are presently already on our journey. At times we even feel our lives have little purpose or meaning. I have not come across one person yet who was not already on a definite path in life. Some knew of their path, while many others were totally unaware that each step they took did have specific meaning.

When I feel confused, lost and scared, I remind myself that this, too, is a part of my path and necessary for my continued growth. Knowing this keeps me grounded, even when all appears to be chaotic — much like the calm in the eye of the hurricane. I would not give up the storms which disrupt my serenity today because I know they are all a part of my path. All of the storms, whirlwinds and tornadoes on your path, as painful as they may be, are a part of your life experience. Boundaries give them definition and clarity.

Good luck to you on your journey. Know your life already has meaning and purpose which is specifically for you and your continued growth.

RESOURCES

Addicts And Family of Addicted

Al-Anon, Al-Anon Adult Children of Alcoholics and
Alateen Family Groups
P.O. Box 862 Midtown Station
New York, NY 10018-086

Alcoholics Anonymous
Box 459
Grand Central Station
New York, NY 10163

Adult Children of Alcoholics
6381 Hollywood Blvd., Suite 685
Hollywood, CA 90028

Cocaine Anonymous
P.O. Box 1367
Culver City, CA 90232

Cult Awareness Network
2421 W. Pratt Blvd., Suite 1173
Chicago, IL 60645

Drugs Anonymous
P.O. Box 473, Ansonia Station
New York, NY 10023

Nar-Anon
P.O. Box 2562
Palo Verdes, CA 90274

Nar-Anon Family Groups
350 5th Street, Suite 207
San Pedro, CA 90731

Pill-Anon Family Programs
P.O. Box 120 Gracie Station
New York, NY 10028

Pills Anonymous
P.O. Box 473, Ansonia Station
New York, NY 10023

Co-dependents Anonymous — Central Office
P.O. Box 5508
Glendale, AZ 85312

National Association for Adult Children of Alcoholics
31582 Coast Highway, Suite B
Laguna Beach, CA 92677

Families

Caregivers Support Groups — Community
Care Resources
(612) 642-4046 — Wilder Foundation

Divorce Anonymous
P.O. Box 5313
Chicago, IL 60680

Families Anonymous
P.O. Box 344
Torrance, CA 90501
(P.O. Box 528, Van Nuys, CA 91409)

Parental Stress Service, Inc.
154 Santa Clara Ave.
Oakland, CA 95610

Parents Anonymous
22330 Hawthorne Blvd.
Torrance, CA 90503

Parents Without Partners
7910 Woodmont Ave.
Washington, DC 20014

Family Violence

Batterers Anonymous
P.O. Box 29
Redlands, CA 92373

Survivors Network
18653 Ventura Blvd., #143
Tarzana, CA 91356

Eating Disorders

Overeaters Anonymous
4025 Spenser Street, Suite 203
Torrance, CA 90503

Food Addicts Anonymous
P.O. Box 057394
West Palm Beach, FL 33405

Sexual Disorders

Sexual Addicts Anonymous
P.O. Box 3038
Minneapolis, MN 55403

CoSA (Co-dependents of Sexual Addicts)
Twin Cities CoSA
P.O. Box 14537
Minneapolis, MN 55414

Incest

Incest Survivors Anonymous
P.O. Box 5613
Long Beach, CA 90805

Sexual Abuse Anonymous
P.O. Box 80085
Minneapolis, MN 55408

Survivors of Incest Anonymous
P.O. Box 21817
Baltimore, MD 21222

Miscellaneous Self-Help Information

Self-Help Center
1600 Dodge Ave.
Evanston, IL 60201

RECOMMENDED READING

Ackerman, Robert J. **Perfect Daughters: Adult Daughters Of Alcoholics.** Deerfield Beach, FL, Health Communications, Inc., 1989.

Becker, Robert. **Addicted To Misery: The Other Side Of Co-dependency.** Deerfield Beach, FL, Health Communications, Inc., 1989.

Boehm, L. "The Development of Independence: A Comparative Study," *Child Development,* 28, pg. 85-92, 1957.

Bradshaw, John. **Bradshaw On: Healing The Shame That Binds You.** Deerfield Beach, FL, Health Communications, Inc., 1988.

Fishel, Ruth. **Time For Joy: Daily Affirmations.** Deerfield Beach, FL, Health Communications, Inc., 1989.

Harlow, H.F. "The Development of Affectional Patterns In Infant Monkeys," in B.M. Foss (ed.) **Determinants Of Infant Behavior.** New York, Wiley, 1961, Vol. 1.

Jung, C.G. "The Stages of Life," in Read, H., Fordham, M., and Adler, G., (ed.) **Collected Works.** Princeton, N.J., Princeton University Press, 1960, Vol. 8.

Miller, Alice. **The Drama Of The Gifted Child.** New York, Basic Books, 1981.

Miller, Joy. **Addictive Relationships: Reclaiming Your Boundaries.** Deerfield Beach, FL, Health Communications, Inc., 1989.

Oliver-Diaz, P. and O'Gorman, Patricia A. **12 Steps To Self-Parenting For Adult Children.** Deerfield Beach, FL, Health Communications, Inc., 1989.

Robinson, Bryan E. **Work Addiction: Hidden Legacies Of Adult Children.** Deerfield Beach, FL, Health Communications, Inc., 1989.

Wills-Brandon, Carla. **Eat Like A Lady: Guide For Overcoming Bulimia.** Deerfield Beach, FL, Health Communications, Inc., 1989.

Wills-Brandon, Carla. **Is It Love Or Is It Sex? Why Relationships Don't Work.** Deerfield Beach, FL, Health Communications, Inc., 1989.

Breinigsville, PA USA
04 August 2010
243073BV00001B/96/A